LESSONS FROM C. S. LEWIS

LESSONS FROM C. S. LEWIS

BECOMING AN EVANGELICAL
APOLOGETIC DISCIPLE FOR CHRIST

Harvey E. Solganick, Ph.D.

Archway Publishing books may be ordered through booksellers or by contacting:

Archway Publishing
1663 Liberty Drive
Bloomington, IN 47403
www.archwaypublishing.com
1 (888) 242-5904

Because of the dynamic nature of the Internet, any web addresses or links contained in this book may have changed since publication and may no longer be valid. The views expressed in this work are solely those of the author and do not necessarily reflect the views of the publisher, and the publisher hereby disclaims any responsibility for them.

This book is a work of non-fiction. Unless otherwise noted, the author and the publisher make no explicit guarantees as to the accuracy of the information contained in this book and in some cases, names of people and places have been altered to protect their privacy.

Any people depicted in stock imagery provided by Getty Images are models, and such images are being used for illustrative purposes only.
Certain stock imagery © Getty Images.

ISBN: 978-1-4808-6159-6 (sc)
ISBN: 978-1-4808-6160-2 (e)

Library of Congress Control Number: 2018904145

Print information available on the last page.

Archway Publishing rev. date: 05/22/2018

I especially dedicate this book to the late Rex Stephens, Wilmington, North Carolina, whose love for C. S. Lewis transformed him and inspired me to reach out to the layperson as well as to my academic colleagues.

You will be both grieved and amused to hear that out of about 60 reviews of *Out of the Silent Planet* only 2 showed any knowledge that my idea of the fall of the Bent One was anything but an invention of my own. But if there only was someone with a richer talent and more leisure I think that this great ignorance might be a help to the evangelization of England; any amount of theology can now be smuggled into people's minds under the cover of romance without their knowing it.

From C. S. Lewis. *The Letters of C. S. Lewis* (July 9, 1939), 167.

CONTENTS

Preface xv

Forward xvii

Introduction... xxi

Chapter 1 The Life of C. S. Lewis: A Journey from *Boxen*
           Land to *Narnia* Land 1

           Recognizing the Sacredness of Life–Birth, Genetics,
           and Abortion... 1
                Family Influences:
                Death of his mother
                The Influence of his Brother, Warnie
                The Loss of Joy, his Wife.............................. 6
                Recapturing the Imagination: Past, Present, and
                Future Faith 6
           Discovering the Early Works of C. S. Lewis.................... 14
                *Boxen 14
                *Letters to Children.................................. 16
                *Dymer 17
           Implications for Evangelism and Discipleship 20

Chapter 2 Youth, Discipleship, Discipline, Education 27

           The Hard Knock from Emotions to Apologetics 27
           Atheism, Agnosticism and Anglicanism........................ 36

Education: The Roots of Discipleship 38

The New Age: Mysticism and Theosophy............................ 39

Toward Theism and Mere Christianity 50

Implications for Evangelism and Discipleship 51

Discovering the Classic Apologetic Works of C. S. Lewis 53

    The Abolition of Man 53

    Miracles 56

    Mere Christianity 58

Chapter 3 Maturity and Adulthood: Salvation and Separation........ 61

Implications for Evangelism and Discipleship 94

Discovering the Works of Heaven (Love and

Reconciliation) and Hell (Divorce and Alienation) 96

    The Four Loves... 96

    The Great Divorce.. 97

    The Screwtape Letters 100

Chapter 4 Evangelism: The Roots of Witnessing with Mere

Christianity.. 102

Discovering the Science-Fiction Works by C. S. Lewis.. 133

    The Science Fiction Trilogy-That Hideous

    Strength, Out of the Silent Planet, Perelandra 133

    Pilgrim's Regress (1930-1940) 133

Chapter 5 Discipleship: The Roots of Becoming a Mature

Christian 134

Living a Literary Life: The Influence of the Christian

Writers—Medievalists and Inklings............................... 136

Apologetics: The Roots of Becoming a Logical

Christian against New Age Theosophy and Secularism 137

Implications for Evangelism and Discipleship 138

Discovering the Works of Christian Reflection by
C. S. Lewis 140
The Problem of Pain,
A Grief Observed,
Surprised by Joy 140

Bibliography 141

ACKNOWLEDGEMENTS

I would like to acknowledge the influence, encouragement, and support from my fellow inklings as we share a love for C. S. Lewis and his works. I was first introduced to the realm of C. S. Lewis by Dr. Martin Batts and encouraged by my colleagues, Dr. Stan Coppinger, at LeTourneau University, Longview, Texas and Dr. Steve Smith, Southwestern Baptist Theological Seminary. The C. S. Lewis and Inklings Society, led by Dr. Salwa Khoddam, and its members, especially Jonathan Himes, John Brown University, Siloam Springs, Arkansas; Dr. Mark Hall, Oral Roberts University, Tulsa, Oklahoma; Dr. Larry Fink, Hardin-Simmons University; Dr. Joe R. Christopher, Tarleton State University, Texas, and Dr. Devin Brown, Ashbury Seminary. The authors who guided me with their personal wit and writings were Dr. John G. West, Discovery Institute C. S. Lewis and Culture Seminar, Seattle, Washington; Dr. Peter Kreeft, Acton University, Grand Rapids, Michigan; and Prof. Jerry Root, Wheaton College. I am grateful for a sabbatical grant from Southwestern Baptist Theological Seminary, Fort Worth, Texas, as well as a C. S. Lewis Fellowship Grant from The Discovery Institute, Seattle, Washington, under the leadership of Dr. John G. West. My gratitude extends to the C. S. Lewis Foundation and the provision of a scholarship to the Oxbridge Summer Institute, England. The spiritual support for writing this book as well as the curriculum for a C. S. Lewis course at Southwestern Seminary I attribute to my Dean, Dr. Mike Wilkinson, and to my colleagues in the Scarborough College Department at Mathena Hall, especially Dr. Keith Loftin, Dr. Donald Kim, Dr. Charles Carpenter, and Dr. Michael Keas. I thank Ryland Whitehorn, executive pastor of First Baptist Church of Dallas and originator of Discipleship University, for allowing me to develop my ideas, teaching a course on C. S. Lewis, Evangelism, and Discipleship. I admire my pastor, Dr. Robert Jeffress, for speaking the truth in love, using apologetics, and quoting C. S. Lewis often in his sermons. Thanks to my publisher, the reviewers, the editors, with the Archway Publishers Division of Simon and Schuster: Randy Clayton, Heather Perry, Zak Helawa, and Gwen Ash. Above all, to my wife, Elaine, I am eternally indebted to her being the Joy Davidman in my life, witnessing to me about Christ, allowing me to find the Joy, escaping from being a liberal, New York, atheist, communist Jew!

PREFACE

After decades of dedicated teaching at Southwestern Baptist Theological Seminary and LeTourneau University, I have been writing and presenting scholarly papers on the works and life of C. S. Lewis. I continued my research on C. S. Lewis from an evangelical perspective concerning his stand on philosophical and ethical issues relevant to evangelical Christians today. I do believe he has influenced many Christians in their preaching and evangelical witness from the pulpit today. He is the most quoted Christian across several Protestant denominations with his wit, insight, and perspectives on Christian issues from life to death and beyond. *Time Magazine* honored him as the most popular Christian with Americans. Collecting my previous publications and presentations as well as new insights from attending libraries, institutes, and visiting places where Lewis composed his works and where scholars have examined his religious stands and issues, I have included a list of publications, presentations, and visitation sites at the end of this study. Issues Lewis explored include marriage, creation, Immaculate Conception, abortion, atheism, behaviorism, and other relevant issues for evangelicals. I plan to trace a biographical sketch of his life from birth to death and beyond, demonstrating specific issues addressed for all of us. For example, in the issue of birth during Lewis' childhood, I will discuss the issue of eugenics, or genetic engineering, predestination, and abortion. In the issue of death, I will address such issues as euthanasia, suicide and immortality. I will provide quotations from Lewis' works addressing these issues, examining the agreements and disagreements with sound doctrine in Christianity, or what we think he meant by

"Mere Christianity." From this research and visit to scholarly sites, I will write some applications on C. S. Lewis and Evangelical Ethics, on his influence from his life and works concerning Christian Apologetics, and on his implications for Discipleship today, demonstrating his agreement and disagreements with evangelical positions at issue today in engaging the postmodern culture. I hope the audiences include not just academics and scholars, but also churches, pastors, homeschooling students, church groups, and youth-adult discipleship training sessions. Most of all, I hope, just as Lewis appealed to the layperson, this book will provide practical wisdom as well as doctrinal clarity. I believe the specific issues raised by Lewis have not been explored by other works on C. S. Lewis, and the reader will be "surprised by joy" with new explorations into the life and work of C. S. Lewis.

Harvey E. Solganick, Ph.D.

FORWARD

Do you ever wonder why C. S. Lewis is so popular with Evangelicals when he is an Anglican? He is the most quoted author by pastors, no matter what denomination. Usually, Pastors or clergy utter one-liners, clichés, and familiar quotes although they have not studied his life, background, theology, or doctrines. *Time Magazine* recognized him as early as 1947 as being the "Don" of Christian Theology. Scholars flock to his Oxford-Cambridge background in the Classics and Medieval Scholarship, to his apologetics in *Mere Christianity,* and to his collection of essays in *God in the Dock.* Children flock to his fairy tales in *The Chronicles of Narnia.* Young adults, including Trekkies, flock to his science-fiction trilogy, *Out of the Silent Planet, Perelandra, and That Hideous Strength.* Romantics seek love in his autobiographies like *A Grief Observed and Surprised by Joy,* but usually accept the pseudo-Hollywood version of the film *Shadowlands* about his love and marriage to Joy Davidman. Other romantic novelists read *Till We Have Faces* as a love story, but are clueless to the mythopoetic, or creative writing of integrating stories, as emphasis in the novel. Those seeking instant advice on love can listen to C. S. Lewis' radio shows on audiobooks like *The Four Loves.* Even those searching for meaning and purpose in life, including new baby Christians, can gleam insights or ammunition against Christianity with his ironic, satiric *The Screwtape Letters.*

How did this one man influence so many readers of all ages and backgrounds, from the most highly educated to the common layperson? Especially, how did this man, his life, and writings help atheists, agnostics, humanists, reluctant converts, mystics, and anti-Christians seek Christ with his doctrine of *Sehnsucht,* God drawing us to him, hidden in mysterious ways in his writings? Perhaps, C. S. Lewis himself went through a search for the soul himself with successive stages and phases in different worldviews during his life, like most of us do in our own lives. Ultimately, Sigmund Freud intrigues me with his search for the Psyche, *Seele,* or Soul, but he lost it, whereas C. S. Lewis finds his soul on the journey from his childhood world of *Boxer* to the mature Christian world of *Narnia.* Perhaps, Lewis can teach us too how to find our souls, be saved, evangelize others, and grow in Christian discipleship. Come with me on a journey through the life of C. S. Lewis, his writings, and you will be surprised by Joy!

In the first Chapter, we will examine the roots of C. S. Lewis' childhood springing toward his imaginative world of fantasy, mythology, and ultimately the foundation for his discovery of the "true myth"- Christianity. The interpersonal relationship with his brother, Warnie, shaped his caring attitude toward others, and his loving relationship with his mother, whom he loses to cancer at an early age, develops a need for seeking reconciling relationships, especially toward Joy Davidman, whom he also loses to cancer, and ultimately to Jesus Christ, the one who will not depart from him. We will explore his first writings, *Boxen,* based upon the animal land he made up with his brother, Warnie, a proto-type for *The Chronicles of Narnia.* His poem, *Dymer,* contains the seeds of his apologetics, his views of science and the Designer of the universe, and his sense of the spirit of life, *Zoe.* Although C. S. Lewis never had biological children in his life, he adopted Joy Davidman's children into his home, and he never gave up his childhood infatuation with fantasy and the creative imagination as evidenced in his later *Letters to Children.* His strong commitment to the sacredness of life becomes the respect for children, birth and a rejection of eugenics, or social biological engineering of genetics, as foundational values for his Christian objection to abortion as well. The works of Lewis, like *The Abolition of Man,* and science-fiction literature, like *Pilgrim's Regress,* become later expressions of his early childhood searching for the meaning of his youth.

In the second Chapter, we learn how Lewis is shaped by his education, especially by the teachings of his headmaster, William T. Kirkpatrick, the hard knock atheist, who taught Lewis logic and how to think with rationality. We see him as the prototype for Professor Kirk in The *Lion, Witch, and Wardrobe* later, who asks "What are they teaching in these schools today?" This step was important in his life since he argues for Christianity as an apologist, using his intellect and logical argumentation, formulating his belief that God exists and the Son of God is Jesus Christ. However, this represents a prevenient, preliminary step toward salvation, through the philosophical ideology of Theism. This phase of his life from adolescence to his Oxford experience represents his search for God continuing through mysticism, theosophy (a magical philosophy of theology based upon supernaturalism), mythology (Lewis studied Greek and Norse myths concerning gods), and other areas until he is convinced logically of "Mere Christianity." Like Lewis, I pursued the Truth in all the wrong places including mysticism and New Age philosophical worldviews but engaging the other worldviews in culture strengthened my faith. I read Marilyn Ferguson's *The Aquarian Conspiracy* and was absorbed into the Oneness of the Cosmos as a New Ager, but fortunately also read Douglas Groothius' *Unmasking the New Age,* challenging the fuzzy beliefs of universality, which Lewis believed also for a while until Reason prevails.

In Chapter Three, we see how Lewis encounters the negative outcomes in his life. The death of his mother and friend in the War, the care for his brother's drinking bouts, his growth toward a rational, Theistic Christianity, his predisposition to being saved by "Thinking Christianly" on the infamous motorcycle ride to the zoo and his absurd, existential conversion parallel to the Zoo Story in Edward Albee's play, simply stating, "I now believe in God and Jesus is the Son of God," as if he were waiting for Godot to show up in natural revelation, discovering God through logical inference from natural observation. In addition, Lewis struggles with his notion of Heaven and Hell and enters into his own hellish nightmare after he tries to marry Joy Davidman under God, a divorced woman in the eyes of The Church. Ultimately, the final struggle of the reluctant convert is his special revelation of the personal relationship with his friends and with the loss of his wife through death, leading to a higher special, personal relationship, and reconciliation with Jesus Christ on a spiritual level.

In Chapter Four, we discover the maturity of Lewis' journey, the application of Christianity in his lifestyle, uniting the mind, heart, and will for discipleship, growing nearer to Christ in his image. Mere Christianity becomes much more than mere Christianity because it is not a list of doctrines taught by the church, nor a set of presuppositions on a logical level, but a lived, personal conviction. The Christian is guided by the Holy Spirit, by the role of the Trinity, and by a sense of communion—community. Lewis rescues the society from the roles of government and scientism in our lives when those roles become unethical and irrational. This doctrine of replacing false science and knowledge becomes Lewis's philosophy against "scientocracy." The applications for Discipleship and Evangelism based upon Lewis' works are explored.

In the concluding Chapter Five, we see how to apply the influence of Lewis' literature and works as well as other Christian literature in spreading the gospel of the good news of Christianity to others, reaching others for Christ in utilizing Christian literature, apologetics, and relational evangelism. Hopefully, this book, this journey, will allow us to spread what Lewis calls "the good infection," the gospel of Jesus Christ so that we can love our neighbors as ourselves and cure the disease in our lives and in our communion-ity.

INTRODUCTION

Biography: "You must be born again" ...

My life story parallels in some ways the life of C. S. Lewis. If you will allow me, as Dr. W.A. Criswell, my first pastor used to say, "to take a leaf out of the pages of my life," I would like to reveal why C. S. Lewis was influential in my becoming a Christian. I was blessed to be born in the U.S.A. but more blessed to be "born again" as a Christian. My parents were immigrants from Eastern Europe and came to the United States as children, escaping the persecution of the Pogroms in Russia as Orthodox Jews in 1914. I was born in 1944 in Brooklyn, New York and moved to Dallas, Texas when I was eight years old, the same time C. S. Lewis was becoming popular with his writings in England and America. I understood how Lewis felt as he and his brother, Warnie, moved from their township in Ireland to a new house, an unfamiliar environment. Watching the reaction of the children in *The Lion, Witch, and Wardrobe*, when they had to move into the new house with the professor during war times, brought back memories of a childhood anxiety in strange new lands. Jack and Warnie created their imaginary world of *Boxen* to return to the naivety of the garden, just as we are restoring the Garden of Eden back to the New Jerusalem to the Lord. The whole advent of technology and progress through science as the new idol of the twentieth century was taking hold by the 1950's, where "progress was our most important product." Lewis viewed the trains and boats and science itself with eugenics in his poem, creating a cruel world in *Dymer*, and later, the war machines and weapons, as means to an end, *The Abolition of Man*. I no longer was in the ghetto of Brooklyn Orthodox Jews but was transported to the Southern Bible belt. God in his wisdom placed me among Christians for my conversion.

My parents' early deaths also opened the door for the Holy Spirit to enter my life. My father was a stern Orthodox Jew who did rear me in the Old Testament and Torah law, giving me a solid religious foundation, so I could return to it in my wayward diversions away from religion. Like Lewis, I pursued other avenues like agnosticism, atheism, mysticism before returning to God's Word. My upbringing in the Old Testament paved the way for understanding the New Testament as a "completed Jew" (although I dislike the term itself, implying there is something incomplete about a child of God's creation). My mother taught me to not only think with the intellect, but with the heart, a value I still cherish as I became a Christian. The two verses I learned were consistent in the Old Testament and in the New Testament: "As a man thinks in his heart, so he is" and "Love the Lord with all your mind, heart, and the power of your soul." It was no accident that my conversion came at a Jewish cemetery where my parents were buried. I asked the Holy Spirit to descend upon me and tell me if Jesus Christ is real. I fell upon my knees and accepted Christ there. The personal experience and relationship with the Lord was what I needed, not more intellectual journeys and diversions. This same process happened to C. S. Lewis as I read *Surprised by Joy* and *A Grief Observed*. While Lewis lost his wife, ironically, Joy Davidman, a New York communist Jew, who converted to Christianity like me, I believe it was his personal loving relationship with Joy growing out of their friendship leading him to the throne of true salvation. Lewis was a reluctant convert, first believing intellectually the teachings of the catechisms of the church, then discarding them for agnostic inquiry, overthrowing them for atheism, pursuing the substitute of mysticism and theosophy as exploration, and then finding the arguments of Theism appealing as logic, rationality, and apologetics describing the natural revelation of God rather than reductionist materialism and naturalism.

In my own journey, I followed in the same footsteps of the "wandering Jew." I sought eclectic philosophical worldviews I could patch together to satisfy my longings (C. S. Lewis calls them *Sehnsucht* or seeking truth). Philosophy, not Theology, became my idol, the queen of the sciences.

Education: "We don't need no education" …Pink Floyd

In my public education, I became studious since I had few friends and most of the students were Christians evangelizing me and praying for me to become a Christian. I even was invited to morning meditations where I could hold hands with other Christians as they prayed for me. I signed my graduation year book with the sarcastic, haughty remark of a chosen, elected favorite son of God: "Roses are red; violets are blue—If it weren't for Jesus Christ, you would all be a Jew." I vowed I would get even by becoming the intellectual nerd of my school and became the president of the Future Teachers of America Chapter. My goal was to become so educated that I could persecute Christians like Saul. Little did I know they were planting the mustard seed for my own conversion and that I would transform into Paul myself when I met my Damascus Road experience in that Jewish cemetery.

In my higher education, I sought the multitude of views for my collection of truths, relative to my personal whims. I discarded any objective, absolute truths, especially the Truth of the Torah, the Holy Bible, and God the Father. My new heroes were Friedrich Nietzsche, Jean-Paul Sartre, Albert Camus, and other Atheistic Humanistic Existentialists, along with atheists like Sigmund Freud, Karl Marx who turned away from Judaism. Ultimately, I wrote my dissertation on *Sigmund Freud's Search for the Psyche-Soul*, intrigued by his rejection of Judaism and search for a new "science." However, I appreciated my atheistic professors for making me think logically and critically just as C. S. Lewis appreciated his atheistic Headmaster, the Hard Knock, Kirkpatrick, who Lewis said was the most influential person in his life, other than J.R.R. Tolkien who prepared his mind for Christianity. I called my professor, Dr. Richard M. Owsley, the Great Owl, since he was as wise to me as an ideal scholar model. I found the laws of logic more valuable than the law of the Torah just as Lewis departed from his catechisms learned in the Anglican Church away from Christianity. We both found Jesus later who came not to abolish the law—but to fulfill it.

Lewis's earlier education was a foundation for his later beliefs. After the death of his mother and father, in 1929, Lewis and brother Warnie were sent to Wynyard, a boarding school in Watford, England. After the death of my mother and father, I discontinued my education at The University of Texas at Austin and enrolled closer at North Texas State University, to care for my brother, Louis, so we could run the family business, Flowerland, in Oak Cliff, Dallas, Texas. It was another God-appointment for me, leaving the Marxist, liberal education in Austin, to a more conservative education in Education, shaping my life vocation and career. I was starting to give up my "Jewish Orthodoxy" already, but C. S. Lewis kept up his church going as an Ulster Protestant, not impressed by the church liturgy, but by the Christian doctrines expressed. Like Lewis, I had my impression of the Torah in rabbinical school but was not impressed by the ritualization of Hebrew chanting and ceremonies. Judaism taught me to fear God in the most negative, thunderbolt sense of punishment for my sins, just as Lewis experienced self-condemnation and legalism, hindering his prayers in a personal relationship with God. Already Christian super-rationalism was restricting Lewis, just as I was restricted in knowing God and what Henry Blackaby calls "experiencing God." In his early education, Lewis read Walter Hilton's *Ladder to Perfection*, and was exposed to his first taste of mysticism, climbing the imperfection of human knowledge to God. Lewis never confessed his sin since he was preoccupied with his fear and imperfection as a rationalist, a confession that led him later to a personal relationship with Christ.

After Charbourgh, Lewis attended Malvern preparatory school. He was exposed to Atheism by his headmaster, William T. Kirkpatrick, the "Great Knock," who made a great impression on Lewis studying many eclectic beliefs, just as my philosophy professors, like the great owl, Richard M. Owsley, taught me to think logically. From this critical thinking stand, Lewis pursued agnosticism, atheism, naturalism, materialism, dualism, mysticism, pantheism, theism, and eventually back to true Christianity. I followed the same pattern in my own life, the journey of the mind in the history of ideas. Along the way, Lewis read George MacDonald's *Phantastes* (1858), ultimately provoking the Christian mystical side of Lewis, what he calls, "baptizing the imagination" with the divine, magical, and ecstatic reality in which we live. My own inquiry into New Age philosophies, like Zen, following the *Aquarian Conspiracy* of Marilyn Ferguson, paranormal and occult happenings, and Hippie mantras, also led me astray from Orthodox Judeo-Christianity. For Lewis, the study of old age myths and mystical worldviews led him away from Christianity's worldviews into the new age worldviews. There is really nothing new with some new age philosophies since they are based upon some of the same philosophical assumptions and systems that Jesus and Paul encounter in that dispensation of time. Here are some of the principles or assumptions of New Age Philosophy:

1. Neo-Platonism: The Greek philosophy that forms or ideas are detached from the body in a supernatural world of ideas where reincarnation takes place, seeking perfection rather than imperfection in this shadow world or copy-cat imitation of the ideal world. The Greek concept of the rational soul allows philosophers to intuit a greater idea than the physical manifestation of that idea. (Plato, The Republic: "The Myth of Er," "The Myth of the Cave") (Plotinus, "Emanational Pantheism")

2. Gnosticism: The secret philosophy that spirits can only be known by a "cult" of believers and that the body is basically an illusion (Docetism).

3. Epicureanism: The Roman philosophy of hedonism, or pleasure seeking. Epicurus believed in a moderate approach to pleasures, not in the modern concept of a "glutton" Epicurean, but one who enjoys the fine art of eating, drinking, and other pleasures.

4. Stoicism: The Roman philosophy of apathy. Epictetus and Aurelius warn people not to engage in any activity beyond the control of their will. The inability to act against the will frustrates the emotions and causes more harm. "It is not your wife; it is a wife, like the broken vase you owned; just replace it if you lose it!"

5. Pyrrhonism or Skepticism: no knowledge was possible as external, objective truth, so doubt ensues, and only experience can be minimally reliable. (Pyrrho, Hume)
6. Pantheism: Nature is worshipped as God or Spirit:
   A. God is only spirit, never incarnate as body, and pervades nature. (Pantheism)
   B. The world itself is entirely divine.
   C. Truth lies within every human; it is attained through states of mystical consciousness, not rationality.
   D. Ethics is relative
   E. Humans are spiritual beings who are gods.
   F. Ignorance of our true human potential is the basic human problem.
   G. The solution to the human problem is transformation of our consciousness.

Lewis attended Oxford University College in 1917, pursuing these ideas of New Age mysticism, but his education was interrupted by World War I where he served for two years. His return to Oxford would eventually lead him to significant friendships with his colleagues and open the door to a higher education of relationships based upon friendship and plant the seeds for his conversion to Christianity.

War and Peace: "War—ugh, what is it good for?
Absolutely nothing!" …Sly and the Family Stones

The World War affected C. S. Lewis immensely. From his childhood experience of fantasy, his romantic notion of boats, airplanes, and trains taking him on a journey to the imaginary, fantasy land *Boxen*, became the adult realization of realism: tanks, bombers, and armory—machines of destruction and death. Death became reality for Lewis, first on the death of his mother from cancer, and later from the death of his friend, Paddy, on the battlefield. Paddy asked Lewis to care for his wife if anything should happen to him, and Lewis did exactly that. He asked his spouse to move in with him, caring for the widow at his house.

I shared the same Romanticism notion of war and peace during the revolutionary period of the sixties. I avoided the draft serving in Vietnam by my deferment of teaching during those times of turmoil. Influenced by the Pacifist Idealism of the hippies, I protested the war in Vietnam as an "unjust war." Of course, now I realize I had no idea what Augustine meant by a just war cause, one that C. S. Lewis understood when he fought in the World War for a reason against tyranny and oppression. Lewis saw the effects of the holocaust of war and understood the just cause of liberation from the oppression of dictators, while I saw television productions of body bags and "causalities of war" in the killing fields of Cambodia, and rebelled without a cause against law and order, the "military-industrial-establishment." Just as Lewis lost his friend, Paddy, in war, I lost several students in my classes I was teaching to the war in Vietnam. Death is the great equalizer of evil in the world of flesh and the devil. I am now thankful that Jesus conquered death's sting and offered eternal life to me. I believe the war and battle scenes in the *Chronicles of Narnia* reflect C. S. Lewis's own battles in war and search for Christianity and peace. My own existential rebellion without a cause and naïve emotional search for love, peace, and truth left me with a void that could only be filled with the love of Christ.

Lewis joined a cadet battalion stationed in Oxford in 1917 where his roommate was his best friend, Edward F. C. "Paddy" Moore. Paddy introduced Lewis to his mother, Mrs. Janie King Moore. The two pledged to care for parents left behind if one of them did not return from the war. In 1918 Paddy was reported dead. When Lewis returned to Oxford in 1919, he completed his studies and went to live with Mrs. Moore. He introduced people to Mrs. Moore as his mother and the two stayed together for over thirty years until her death in 1951. Mrs. Moore's brother, John, had a fascination for the occult and paranormal, and suffered a psychological collapse in 1923. Lewis then quit his flirtation with the occult returning to the path of Christianity. For Lewis, good and evil were spiritual forces explained by mystical Idealism, but he needed a rational foundation for these beliefs. Like Lewis, I journeyed to Stonehenge and Averbury Circle, seeking King Arthurian legends and the holy grail. Then I took a hippie bus tour with fellow seekers to Zen Buddhist monasteries, like Bodhi New Mexico, and Gary Snyder's commune in California, seeking the "truths" of becoming One with Nature. I turned later to the literary movements, more intellectual for my philosophical tastes: American Transcendentalists, Rosicrucians, Theosophists, and German Romantics like Boehme and Goethe. Lewis and I were both transcendental, rational, organicists, seeking the Oneness of Nature as a nature, mystic deity. For Lewis it leads to his natural revelation preceding his special revelation of Jesus Christ in his life. By God's grace, our mystical bent turned straight to the Bible and God's Word: "Since the creation of the world God's invisible qualities— his eternal power and divine nature—have been clearly seen, being understood from what has been made" (Romans 1:20). The mystical light and Romantic Enlightenment are fused in God's pure Light.

Christian Conversion: "What a Friend we have in Jesus"

From C. S. Lewis's friendship with Paddy on the battlefield to his Platonic friendships in Oxford, Cambridge, and the Kilns homeland, Lewis experienced intellectual challenges as well as interpersonal relationships leading him on the journey to the Lord. Of course, his lifelong friend was his brother, Warnie, who took him on that famous motorcycle ride to the zoo, when Lewis declared he understood now that Jesus Christ is the Son of God. I believe that revelation was a natural revelation based upon his inquiries intellectually with Nature, against reductionist materialism and atheism, a failure of mysticism and Theosophy, and a movement toward Theism, based upon his reasoning and rationalism. Lewis does not become a totally convicted Christian with special revelation until the death of his dearest friend, Joy Davidman, who shared a Platonic love with him and ultimately a spiritual bonding under Christ when they are married. Through the dark night of the soul, Lewis loses his wife to the battle with cancer, just like his mother, but realizes the "problem of pain" losing her is like Christ suffering on the cross for his salvation. The film based upon the play, *Shadowlands*, is a great visual portrayal of this revelation. Thus, all his friends are evangelists, sharing the gospel with Lewis, directly or indirectly. Even his disagreements with his friends lead him to a stronger belief in Christ. It takes great faith to be an atheist, and Christ came into the world to save sinners. Like Lewis I experienced that journey intellectually looking for Christ in all the wrong places. I needed friends for guidance, even atheists and mystics in my own journey.

Like C. S. Lewis, my philosophical studies led me to several degrees in higher education. I completed two master's degrees in liberal arts, and certificates of study at Heidelberg, Germany in Philosophy, including Mittelstufe and Oberstufe certification, and then continued to my doctorate in Philosophy and Humanities at The University of Texas from 1968-1998. My Master's degree prepared me in Liberal Arts, while Lewis's First-Class degree in Oxford afforded him several fields, including classics, ancient philosophy, and English literature from

1920-1923. I studied the same liberal arts background as Lewis. While Lewis studied Norse mythology, I studied Germanic fairy tales and legends, culminating in the study of Bruno Bettelheim's interpretation of Grimm's fairy tales upon children's' psyches. Both Lewis and I were intrigued with myths but were missing what he later calls "the myth made true," Christianity. Lewis and I, both "reluctant converts," had to undergo several phases of transformations or "conversions" in our lives, preparing us for the personal revelation of Jesus Christ as our true Savior. In *Surprised by Joy* (1955), Lewis described two conversion experiences, the first a generalized, intellectual Theism and the second, an acknowledgement that Jesus Christ was God from heaven, the God who died on the cross for others, not for Himself, as Lewis studied in Norse mythology. The first step toward conversion was more mystical, attracted to Christian friends he met at Oxford, J.R.R. Tolkien, Owen Barfield, Charles Williams, William Dyson, and Dorothy Sayers. They witnessed to him intellectually and opened his mind to the possibility of accepting Christianity as a step forward from Theism. The second step toward his conversion was precipitated while riding on the top deck of an omnibus, observing nature around him, avoiding words and mental images, and realizing he was shutting out a revelation of Christ. He continued reading texts like *Phantastes, Diary of an Old Soul, and Lilith* by George MacDonald, John Bunyan's *Grace Abounding*, Dante's *Paradiso*, Jacob Boehme's *The Signature of Things*, Brother Lawrence's *The Practice of the Presence of God*, Thomas Traherne's *Centuries of Meditations*, William Law's *An Appeal to All Who Doubt*, and Thomas a' Kempis's *Imitation of Christ*, as well as the *Gospel of John* in the original Greek. The third preparation toward his conversion is the one most scholars agree was his ultimate conversion to Christ in 1931. During a walk, J.R.R. Tolkien and Dyson persuaded him in a conversational witness that Christ's incarnation is the historical embodiment of the dying god myth, the universal story of One who gives himself for the sake of his people. Then, while riding to the zoo in the sidecar of his brother Warnie's motorcycle, Lewis acknowledged that Christ is God. However, I believe this progressive preparation, from competing Atheism, from

Theism, from Mysticism, from Natural General Revelation, all leads him to the ultimate revelation, a special salvation relationship with Jesus Christ as a special personal revelation of God's Love. Lewis is reconciled to the Trinity after his personal relationship, finding love with his wife, Joy Davidman, and losing that life of love, transforming Lewis into not a mere Christian intellectually and rationally, but into the true truth of a personal relationship with Christ, a friend who will never depart him and always love him.

Love and Marriage: "Love and Marriage go
together like a horse and carriage."

C. S. Lewis experienced the love of friendship from many people during his life. His brother Warnie and he shared *phileo*, or brotherly love together, caring for one another, even in adverse circumstances. Lewis shared comradeship with his military friend Paddy and suffered the loss of his friend to the War. Lewis cared for Paddy's mother and treated her like his own mother out of love. He also continued the love of his mother who died early in his childhood from cancer and always sought the love of his father who did not know how to demonstrate his love for his son except by sending him off to grammar school away from him. Lewis sought mystical love in Theosophy and other explorations into occult mystical ideas, even adhering to Charles Williams idea of the "coinheritance of the Trinity." He sparred with his atheistic headmaster, William T. Kirkpatrick, whom he loved also as a man who taught him to think. At Oxford and Cambridge, he continued his *phileo* love with the Inklings, a group of scholars who were witnessing intellectually to him about Christianity, including J.R.R. Tolkien, Chesterton, Charles Williams, Hugo Dyson, and Dorothy Sayers, as he moved toward Theism. However, the strongest phileo love Lewis experienced was his growing relationship with Joy Davidman, soon growing into a harmonious love, including *Eros, phileo*, and most importantly the *agape* love he would learn in the bond of marriage between God, Joy, and Lewis himself. These progressive stages prepared Lewis for a true conversion, a revelation of Jesus Christ as a personal savior who would never leave him nor forsake him, even after he could not see his wife's face anymore and even after the ideas he sought as a reluctant convert would escape him as transitory vapors in this world. Lewis ultimately took the leap of faith in marrying Joy Davidman, not for a civil ceremonial reason, but for a spiritual reason, and he ultimately took the leap of faith accepting Jesus Christ as a personal relationship throughout eternity. He found the Joy he was seeking with *"Sehnsucht,"* first drawing near to his friends, then to his marriage partner, and ultimately into a personal relationship with

Christ. Lewis was a stubborn horse fighting the bridle of Christ, but his marriage to Joy brings him to the wedding carriage with Christ guiding the reigns, and Lewis winds up as the "bride of Christ" by being saved.

In many ways, my conversion came about through the hardships and struggles intellectually until I met my soulmate, my wife Elaine, the Joy Davidman in my life. Ironically, the roles were reversed. I was the "commie, New York Jew" when I met Elaine. Her name means "Light" and I received the witness of the gospel by her evangelizing and discipleship before we were married. My own testimony is a record of my searching for God in philosophical circles. Like Lewis, I learned from the "hard knock" of atheists, mystics, and agnostics along the way as a preparation for Christianity. I studied secular philosophies of Naturalism, Atheism, Existentialism, Materialism, and then moved into mystical, occult, and Idealistic philosophies of the New Age. As my mentor, the late W.A. Criswell, pastor of the church where I was saved, used to say, "Please allow me to take some of the pages of the leaves of my life and share them with you." Jerry Root at Wheaton College once told me, Lewis believed the three areas that a Christian need are authority, reason, and experience. I will share my own experiences for my salvation, sanctification, and share the glory Christ has given me in my own soul journey:

On a mission trip to Russia for Campus Crusades for Christ in 1998, I was lecturing some students at Moscow University, wondering, "There but for the grace of God, go I." My parents were born in Russia and Rumania, immigrated to Brooklyn, New York, in 1914, under persecution as Orthodox Jews. I was blessed to be born in the U.S.A. My father worked in the shipyards, welding, while also playing in a band at night, to provide for his family. Being poor, he hocked his saxophone and gave up a music career, while my mother worked in the sewing sweatshops of New York City. Both my mother and father only had about an 8th grade education, never achieving graduation or college. However, they wanted their son to achieve a better life and supported my first years of education later. Opportunity knocked, and my parents and I moved to Dallas, Texas (in the Bible belt!), where my Uncle offered my father a position at his flower shop in Oak Cliff. Eventually, my father owned his own store, and I worked there, as a salesman and accountant all through my high school days at Sunset High School.

Even as I worked in the business world, I felt a calling to teach. I was president of the Future Teachers of America in my high school. My favorite teachers were Mrs. Hattie Hornbeck, an appropriate name for an English teacher, and Coach Byron Rhome, whose son, Jerry, broke school records for passing in football. All the teachers and students were Christians, asking me to pray with them at morning meditations. I rejected Christians, assuming I was already chosen to be saved. As I left for college after graduation from high school, I also left my Judaism behind. Entering The University of Texas at Austin, a whole new world of philosophies opened up to me. I had only studied The Old Testament in Hebrew School and gave up my studies after my Bar Mitzvah. I rejected an awesome, fearsome God for a humanistic belief in people's secular values. I believed in a liberal, open selection of eclectic worldviews for everyone. There was one worldview I could not tolerate, however, and that view was Christianity. Christianity seemed too exclusive and not inclusive enough for an intellectual mind-seeker like me. Thus, I studied the New Testament to "put it down." But, God works in mysterious ways. I started noticing the parallels and prophecies in the Old Testament with the New Testament (especially, in the Book of Isaiah 53: "By His stripes, you shall know Him."[1]). Then, death, the final fate, occurred in the passing away of my mother and father.

As I worked in my father's flower shop after graduation with my brother, I continued my education at North Texas State University in Denton. When I graduated with my bachelor's degree in English and Philosophy, I began teaching at Duncanville High School. My brother took over the flower shop, and soon it was sold. I continued

---

[1] All Scriptures are taken from the version of *The Holman Christian Standard Bible* (Nashville: Holman Publishers, 2004) unless otherwise noted. Lewis himself read modern translations of Dr. Moffatt and Monsignor Knox of the King James Authorized Version of the Holy Bible. I am indebted to Dr. Roger White, Curator of Special Collections and Rare Books at the Azusa Pacific University Library for his research.

my master's degree in education at The University of North Texas while teaching, and I finished another master's degree in liberal arts at S.M.U. in Dallas. My career turned toward community college teaching, and I accepted positions at Texarkana College, Tarrant County Junior College, and at Eastfield College of Dallas County Community College District. Still teaching humanistic philosophy courses, I began to see the shortcomings and failures of the intellectual pursuit of the philosopher's worldview (Romans 8:23: "We all fall short of the glory of God."). Living in Heidelberg, Germany, at the only room I could find at the Theologische Haus (Theology House) on a grant, I studied even more German humanistic philosophies, visiting Philosopher's Hill, but there I met some evangelical Christians. I had wrongly assumed all Christians were not intellectual and using their minds. When I returned to the U.S.A. after my certification in doctoral German studies, I attended the First Baptist Church in Dallas, and heard the sermons of W.A. Criswell, and other powerful preachers, who knew the Word of God, both intellectually and passionately. I met a wonderful woman there, a former student of mine, who asked me to return to Church with her on a consistent basis. God had brought us together, but we were not ready to be together yet ("Do not be yoked to an unbeliever!").

It was a dark, dreary day at the Jewish cemetery in 1988, as I looked down at my parents' graves. I wondered, *do I want to be there in the grave without knowing Jesus Christ?* The Holy Spirit descended upon me, and I accepted Jesus Christ as my Savior, the true Messiah. Like the apostle Paul's Damascus experience, the light dawned upon me. From that point on, I began studying God's Word, joined a Messianic congregation for Jewish believers, and then totally immersed myself in Baptism at the First Baptist Church of Dallas. I attended Criswell College, and Dallas Theological Seminary, and received my certificate of Biblical Studies. Although my Jewish family relatives disowned me, held a funeral for me, my new family as a new creature in Christ was warmly accepting me. I felt all the joy of Christianity by a loving, graceful God. However, I soon learned when James says, "Call it all joy in your suffering," and when the Beatitudes in Matthew state, "Blessed are the persecuted, for theirs will be the kingdom of God." My secular teaching was accepted, but my spiritual teaching was rejected.

The community college administration persecuted my openness to God in the classroom, even though I never proselytized, nor even mentioned Jesus. They were fearful of my walk with the Lord, the transformation coming over me, and the ACLU! They began reducing my salary for professional advancement and other actions. I decided to take a "leap of faith." I saw an advertisement for part-time Adjuncts in the newspaper for Dallas Baptist University, Dallas Christian College, and for LeTourneau University. I taught all over town, so I could have the opportunity to pray and mention God and Jesus in the classroom, integrating faith and learning. I continued my studies and received my Ph.D. in Philosophy, Rhetoric, and Humanities at The University of Texas at Arlington, writing a dissertation on why Freud lost his soul because of the lack of evangelical preaching in Germany. Finally, a full-time position opened at Missouri Baptist College of St. Louis, and I taught there for three years, commuting back to Dallas on the weekends to be with my helpmate, that same woman who waited upon me to become a true believer before becoming my wife, and my guide for maturing as a Christian. Then God opened the opportunity to be a full-time professor at the main campus of LeTourneau University, then Missouri Baptist University, and ultimately The Scarborough College at Southwestern Baptist Theological Seminary. I learned to serve the Lord, serve the students, and grow in the mind of Christ. Thus, I had to leave my human pursuit of philosophies, the secular university, and even the country, to allow the Holy Spirit to convert me. My life verse from God's Word has guided me: "Come, now, let us reason together, so your sins of scarlet shall be as white as snow" (Isaiah 1:18).

Death and Renewal: Beyond the Shadowlands to Narnia

Thus, like Lewis, I experienced the problem of pain with the loss of my parents, and even observed my grief when my New York family disowned me and buried me as if I were dead when I became a Christian. But also, like Lewis, I was surprised by the joy for my new found Christian life as a new creature in Christ with a new family, the church, who loves me. When I first read C. S. Lewis, I realized how parallel our lives were and how much God loved us by sending his Son, Jesus, and I knew I wanted to share the gospel evangelically with all through my teaching and writing, but most of all, personally, and disciple believers to grow stronger in the image of God through his Son, Jesus Christ, until death do us part and we are absent with the body and present with the Lord. I realized Lewis had gone through deprivation of his loved ones, rejection by his family and friends, but not forsaking the love of Christ in his life. I hope this journey through Lewis's life and works will influence you evangelically and to continue your discipleship through his influence.

CHAPTER 1

The Life of C. S. Lewis: A Journey from *Boxen* Land to *Narnia* Land

Early Childhood: Recognizing the Sacredness of Life–Birth, Genetics, and Abortion

We begin our journey in the garden of C. S. Lewis' boyhood home, Little Lea, Belfast, Ireland. Just as the Bible begins the story of humanity with Adam and Eve in the Garden of Eden, Lewis created a wonderful world of fantasy called Animal-Land with his brother, Warren. Both boys moved with their parents, Albert and Flora Lewis, to their new home in 1905, after "Jack" was born in Belfast, November 29, 1898. Being born was a sacred moment for Lewis in his later reflections as an adult since eugenics and abortion become modern ethical principles for him in opposition to the power of Scientism, in the hands of the politicians and scientists. Eugenics is the biological engineering of genes, selecting behavioral traits of a baby, modifying the personality and strengthening the genes of a human being with as little defects as possible in health and deterministic behavior. Orwell and Aldous Huxley write about these "test-tube babies" in the novels, *1984* and *Brave New World*. B.F. Skinner advocated programming humans through behavioral reinforcement in the psychology of behaviorism in his book *Beyond Freedom and Dignity*, based upon the animalistic stimulus-response theory of Watson. C. S. Lewis directly views the outcomes of unethical biological manipulation of humans in Hitler's war. As early as his writing of *Dymer*, Lewis is approaching the dangers of a political society built upon social engineering or eugenics. He continues this theme throughout his writings as a warning to the end of mankind. Lewis dreaded "government in the name of scientific technocracy."[2] For Lewis, Freudian psychological scientists assume we live as a bundle of complexes. Marxists state we exist as members of a scientifically determined economic class. Science combined with eugenics turns earth into a heaven with false idealism, the work of the devil: "So inveterate is their appetite for Heaven that our best method, at this stage, of attaching them to Earth, is to make them believe that Earth can be turned into Heaven at some future date by politics or eugenics or "science" or psychology or what not."[3] The sacredness of life was imminent in birth, during the war, and as he saw beloved family and friends dying in his lifetime. As Lewis develops the journey of *Dymer* away from his "perfect" social-engineered society, *Dymer* dares through his independent dream to discover his identity, but loses it to the "curse of madness":

> There is a city which men call in scorn/The Perfect City—eastward of this wood—You've heard about this place. There I was born. I'm one of them, their work. Their sober mood, The ordered life, the laws, are in my blood—A life…well, less than happy, something more/ Than the red greed and lusts that went before… Then-how or why it was, I cannot say—this Dymer, this fool baby pink-and-white, / Went mad beneath his quiet face…[4]

C. S. Lewis struggles with the ethical choices people must make, but he never oversteps his own philosophy by forcing it upon others.

---

[2] C. S. Lewis, "Bulverism or the Foundation of 20th Century Thought." In *God in the Dock*. Ed. Walter Hooper. (Grand Rapids: Eerdmans,1970), 299-304.
[3] C. S. Lewis, *The Screwtape Letters* (New York: Collier Macmillan,1982), 133.
[4] C. S. Lewis, *Dymer*, Canto 15;17. (London: J.M. Dent Publications. Distributed by Macmillan, 1926), 41.

He assumes each person will make a rational choice given the truth of the matter.

The same case holds for ethical dilemmas like abortion. Although Lewis is convicted with the sacredness of life since ironically the devils in *Screwtape* believe a false doctrine in response to the sacredness of life, "In God's view, human birth is important, chiefly as qualification for human death which is the gate to heaven."[5] However, Lewis does not have a clear argument for or against abortion on the grounds first that he is not a woman: "I am not a woman—I did not think it my place to take a firm line without pains, dangers and expenses from which I am protected."[6] On one hand, for a second reason, Lewis is ambivalent about retribution or sin becoming a crime in matters like homosexuality or abortion: "No sin simply as such, should be made a crime. Who are the rulers to enforce their opinions of sin on us? Of course, many acts or sins against God are also injuries to our fellow citizens and must on that account only be made crimes."[7] At least Lewis recognizes, on the other hand, the higher ethical judgement from God involved in the sacredness of life, developed as *Zoe* or the Life-Force in Mere Christianity. Ultimately, birth itself is the beginning of a journey to death and then to resurrection of the body, but the pain of childbirth is a necessary transition:

> "Birth is likened to a Christian renewal, just as an ordinary baby might, if he had the choice, might prefer to stay in the warmth and safety of the womb."[8] Again, Lewis does not want to infringe his beliefs upon even the birth of a baby, since the church has taken a strong position against birth control as well: "It is not my place; I have said nothing...I am not prepared to say birth

---

[5] C. S. Lewis, *Screwtape Letters,* 133-34.

[6] C. S. Lewis, *Mere Christianity* (New York: Macmillan Publishing Company, 1952), 9.

[7] C. S. Lewis, *Letters of C. S. Lewis* (New York: Harcourt Brace Jovanovich, 1966), February 1958, 281.

[8] C. S. Lewis, *Mere Christianity,* 187.

control is always wrong."[9] However, the foundational principle of the sacredness of life is a standard upheld eventually by Lewis: "I have even (I'm afraid) caught myself wishing that I had never been born, which is sinful. Also, meaningless, if you think it out."[10] It is acceptable to doubt your existence, but then it is not rational to remain in that doubt state long since God must have a purpose, a plan for us being born; otherwise, it is an existential meaningless life, not a "wonderful life." Lewis trusts his rational mind to examine the essence of life itself, birth and death, and what lies beyond.

Although Lewis, or Jack as he was called, during his childhood, loved the trains and boats of his home, it was the natural revelation of God's creation, the land, appealing to him and his imagination. These lands become the fantastic worlds of *Boxen*, combining the lands of Animal-Land and India in his drawings, and the animals surrounding his home become the major characters in his first novel, *Boxen*. Later, Lewis writes in *Surprised by Joy* (1955) about his home and the outdoors of nature:

> To a child it seemed less like a house than a city...The New House is a major character in my story. I am a product of long corridors, empty sunlit rooms, upstairs indoor silences, attics explored in solitude, distant noises of gurgling cisterns and pipes, and the noise of wind under the tiles...Out of doors was the 'view' for which, no doubt the site had principally been chosen. From our front door we looked down over wide fields to Belfast

---

[9] C. S. Lewis, *Mere Christianity,* 9; *Letters,* (March 1956), 268.
[10] C. S. Lewis, *Letters,* (May 1939).

Lough and across it to the long mountain line of the Antrim shore.[11]

No doubt, the reader of *The Lion, Witch, and Wardrobe and The Magician's Nephew* can see the foreshadowing of the professor's house with its corridors and wardrobe in the attic as well as the animals in his work. For the child, the home is a promise of a greater home in heaven, for "In my dwelling place, there are many rooms" (John 14:2 HCSB), a joyful promise of a better home to come, one which Lewis would seek after his home becomes not a joyful place, but a suffering place with the death of his mother in 1908 and his being sent off to boarding school. Lewis remembers his loss of his mother to cancer in *Surprised by Joy*:

> With my mother's death all settled happiness, all that was tranquil and reliable, disappeared from my life. There was to be much fun, many pleasures, many stabs of Joy, but no more of the old security. It as sea and islands now; the great continent had sunk like Atlantis.[12]

His mother's love would affect him throughout his life's journey, spiritually hungering for love, finding it in his wife, Joy Davidman, but again losing it to cancer. It is not until his acceptance of the love of Christ that Lewis finds his true Joy, recognizing the suffering Jesus underwent on the cross, conquering sin and death, for the "wages of sin is death" (Romans 6:23 HCSB). C. S. Lewis indeed is on the journey, the Roman Road to salvation, for the evangelist who offers the gospel:

All have sinned. (Romans 3:23 HCSB)
The wages of sin is death. (Romans 6:23 HCSB)
The good news of the Gospel is that Jesus died
for your sin. (Romans 5:8 HCSB)

---

[11] C. S. Lewis, *Surprised by Joy* (New York: Macmillan, 1955), 10.
[12] C. S. Lewis, *Surprised by Joy*, 21.

You can have everlasting life if you accept Jesus as
your savior and Lord. (Romans 10:13 HCSB)

*Family Influences: Death of his mother; Relationship with brother Warnie;
the Joy of his wife, Joy*

From his mother, C. S. Lewis learned about love and caring for
others. The great wisdom of the teachings of Jesus were taught to Lewis
by his mother, the daughter of a minister: "Love the Lord your God and
love your neighbor as you love yourself. On these two commandments
hang the whole" (Matthew 22:39-40 HCSB). This caring attitude
extended to the mother of Paddy, his friend whom he lost during the War
and promised he would care for his mother. Lewis moved his mother
into his own house. In addition, Lewis cared for his alcoholic brother,
Warnie throughout his life. Finally, his love for Joy Davidman grew as
his understanding of her Jewish-Christian background opened a witness
to C. S. Lewis, a witness brought to him by her relational evangelism,
allowing him to grow into theology and discipleship, away from atheism,
naturalism, materialism, mysticism, and theism, into a true truth, a true
personal revelation of Jesus Christ. Lewis returned to his first love, Jesus,
and the doctrines reinforcing his "mere Christianity" from the church
teachings in his childhood.

Recapturing the Imagination: Past, Present, and Future Faith

By the time C. S. Lewis completes his journey in life, he realizes
the pretenses of his academic life and returns to a boyhood recapturing
of the imagination. He becomes "baptized with the imagination" by
reading George Macdonald's work in fantasy. As a literary critic, a
philosopher, an apologist, a mystic, and a theologian, Lewis realizes he
is not even approaching the throne of Christ. What Lewis recognizes is
the journey of discovery in the mind, the questioning of doctrines and
ideas. C. S. Lewis points out in a footnote in *English Literature of the*

16th Century that "When Judas hanged himself, he had not been reading Calvin."[13] The Protestant doctrines "were not of terror but of joy and hope, and those very troublesome problems and very dark solutions were astonishingly absent from the thought of the first Protestants."[14] According to Lewis, Calvin goes "from the original Protestant experience of conversion to build a system, to extrapolate, to raise all the dark questions and give without flinching the dark answers."[15] The dark observations of total depravity would render us in our ideas of goodness counting for nothing.[16] He was concerned that Modernist Christians would maintain, as stoutly as Calvin, that "there's no reason why God's dealings should appear just or merciful to us."[17] Lewis never considered himself to be a systematic theologian, but one led by Christ, preoccupied with Him alone.

Lewis was one not committed to a denomination as much as one committed to the historic Christian faith. He described himself as "a very ordinary layman of the Church of England, not especially "high" and not especially "low." He was baptized in the Church of Ireland in 1899 and later, after his conversion, joined the Church of England, both Anglican. Anglicans have historically accepted the Bible as the sole criterion in matters of dogma. The Apostles' Creed and the Nicene Creed are the accepted statements of the faith. Anglicans hold the sacraments, including baptism and communion in high esteem, as outward and visible signs of inward and spiritual grace, given by Christ by which we receive that grace. The church also believes in apostolic succession through bishops. However, Lewis was not afraid to voice disagreements with his church. He criticized high Anglicanism and the drift toward the theological liberalism in Anglicanism, including a proposal for women

---

[13] C. S. Lewis, *English Literature in the Sixteenth Century excluding Drama* (Cambridge: Oxford Clarendon Press, 1944: Vol.4), 35.

[14] C. S. Lewis, *English Literature*, 35.

[15] C. S. Lewis, *English Literature*, 42.

[16] C. S. Lewis, *Christian Reflections* (Grand Rapids, Eerdmans Publishing Company, 1967), 62.

[17] C. S. Lewis, *Letters of C. S. Lewis* (New York: Harcourt Brace Jovanovich, 1966), February 18, 1940.

priests. Although he insisted on going to church, he detested some
Anglican services as a zoo. Some scholars, ironically, believe Lewis was
saved on a motorcycle ride on the way to the zoo. Protestants, including
myself, do not always agree with his beliefs like transubstantiation in
communion or in apostolic succession. For example, he was committed
to transubstantiation in the communion, but never explained the
mysticism behind it. Lewis called himself a Christian not given to isms.
The church united stands against sectarianism, "called to be spread out
through all time and space and rooted in eternity, terrible as an army
with banners." [18]

Thus, Lewis would refute any kind of Calvinistic predestination
of wrath as a troubled time for the church and would rather emphasize
the eternity of being with Christ as a joyful longing. In fact, Lewis at
his conversion did not believe in eternal life, but simply came to God
in obedience: "I now number that (eternity) among my greatest mercies
(God was simply to be obeyed because He was God)". [19] Lewis viewed
theological disputes about eternity as restricting the appetite for God
(*Sehnsucht*). He believed in God for a whole year before any belief in the
future life was given to him since hope for eternal life is a "Christian
virtue rather than a form of escapism or wishful thinking."[20] For Lewis,
there is a "divine tact for training the *chosen race* for centuries before
even hinting at eternal life."[21] God is the endless present of eternity, not
merely an older time.[22]

How did C. S. Lewis then view the Jewish question, the nature of

---

[18] Diana Pavlac Glyer, "Anglicanism." *C. S. Lewis Reader's Encyclopedia* (Grand
Rapids: Zondervan, 1998) 80-1.
[19] C. S. Lewis, *Surprised by Joy* (New York: Harcourt, Brace Jovanovich, 1955), 231;
Also, C. S. Lewis, *Reflections on Psalms* (New York: Harcourt, Brace, Jovanovich,
1958), 42.
[20] C. S. Lewis, *Mere Christianity*, Chapter III (New York: Macmillan Publishing
Company, 1952), 118.
[21] C. S. Lewis, *God in the Dock* (Grand Rapids: Eerdmans Publishing Company,
1970), 131.
[22] C. S. Lewis, *Letters to Malcolm: Chiefly on Prayer* (New York: Harcourt, Brace
Jovanovich, 1964), 110.

Israel, and eschatological or future role of the church? Like Calvin and Luther, Lewis's views about Jews and the role of the church progressed from negative to positive views after his conversion. After being exposed to the Messianic Christianity of his wife, a commie, New York Jew like myself, Joy Davidman, Lewis reassessed his views: "I wonder will you ever get to the end of the Bible; the undesirable "primitives" around you will enable you to appreciate the Hebrews who were class A primitives after all."[23] Lewis admires the Israelites later for their "Hebraic background, for which I envy you".[24] Lewis claims the progressive dispensation of the Jews for the fulfillment of the revelation of God himself: "I think it to myself, to remind all us Gentile Christians—who forget it easily enough and even flirt with anti-Semitism—that the Hebrews are spiritually *senior* to us, that God *did* entrust the descendants of Abraham with the first revelation of Himself".[25] Lewis raises the philosophical question, "Why did God not teach the Jewish people earlier about eternal life?"[26] One must pursue the theological answers about eternity, not merely "feel the presence of God in flowers or music."[27] Even the demons know humans live in time but God destines them to eternity.[28] Lewis recognizes the essence of freedom in the actuality of the present moment when eternity touches us as an offering, but we never see the entire "game" plan of God: "One sometimes wonders why God thinks the game worth the candle; but we have not yet seen the game."[29]

One reason why Lewis is not caught up in the eschatological, futuristic arguments is his lack of a systematic and doctrinal theology of the Bible, relying upon the earlier teachings of the church creeds. Although Lewis often quotes the Bible to support his logic or apologetics, he rarely relies upon theological doctrines being developed, but rather

---

[23] C. S. Lewis, *Letters of C. S. Lewis,* 1921, 58.
[24] C. S. Lewis, *Letters of C. S. Lewis* (April 10, 1941), 193.
[25] C. S. Lewis, *Letters of C. S. Lewis* (May 14, 1955), 263.
[26] C. S. Lewis, *Reflections on Psalms,* 39-42.
[27] C. S. Lewis, *Mere Christianity,* Chapter IV,136.
[28] C. S. Lewis, *Screwtape Letters* (New York: Macmillan Publishing Company, 1959), 67.
[29] C. S. Lewis, *Letters to Malcolm,* 91.

common sense, wit, and practicality in his arguments. His temperamental Irish background and personality fit his style of rhetoric, often sounding direct and brash, like many Texans, stiff-necked Jewish people, and New Yorkers I know. Lewis also did not believe the entire Bible was the inerrant, inspired Word of God as I do: Shortly before he died, Lewis commented in *Reflections on the Psalms*, that Christians "still believe (as I do) that all Holy Scripture is in some sense—*though not all parts of it in the same sense*—the Word of God." When it came to the first book of the Bible, *Genesis*, Lewis said, "I have therefore no difficulty in accepting, say, the view of those scholars who tell us that the account of Creation in Genesis is derived from earlier Semitic stories which were Pagan and mythical." (It's important to note that for Lewis, "myth" is not a deception, but an imaginative way of transferring truth. He calls Christianity, "The Myth made real."[30]) Again, Lewis is pragmatic on atonement or Christ's journey to the cross as a substitute for our human sins. Many Christians have strong and specific views on what Christ's sacrifice means and what it accomplished. Lewis, however, seemed to be vaguer. In *Mere Christianity*, Lewis admitted not knowing how the atonement worked: "The central Christian belief is that Christ's death has somehow put us right with God and given us a fresh start. Theories as to how it did this are another matter. A good many different theories have been held as to how it works; what all Christians are agreed on is that it does work."[31] Lewis again does not commit to an understanding of hell, but strongly believes in heaven. It is uncertain whether the British writer believed, as many conservative Christians do, that hell is a place of eternal and conscious punishment for the damned or if Lewis believed in annihilation—that those who go to hell eventually cease to exist after paying for their sins. In *The Problem of Pain*, Lewis wrote the following:

> Destruction...means the unmaking, or cessation, of the destroyed. And people often talk as if the 'annihilation' of a soul were intrinsically possible. In all our experience...

---

[30] C. S. Lewis, *Surprised by Joy*, 235.
[31] C. S. Lewis, *Mere Christianity*, 58-9.

the destruction of one thing means the emergence of something else. Burn a log, and you have gases, heat and ash. To have been a log means now being those three things. If soul can be destroyed, must there not be a state of having been a human soul? And is not that, perhaps, the state which is equally well described as torment, destruction, and privation? You will remember that in the parable, the saved go to a place prepared for them, while the damned go to a place never made for men at all. To enter heaven is to become more human than you ever succeeded in being in earth; to enter hell, is to be banished from humanity. What is cast (or casts itself) into hell is not a man: it is "remains."[32]

He goes onto say, "That the lost soul is eternally fixed in its diabolical attitude we cannot doubt: but whether this eternal fixity implies endless duration—or duration at all—we cannot say."[33] The closed description to hell is based on Dante's vision of *Inferno*, with its levels of rejection and deprivation of love, an alienation from God. Lewis ends his work, *A Grief Observed*, with a quote from Dante: "Beatrice whom he loved dearly looked away from Virgil but looked toward the eternal fountain." Lewis's painful travels through life including his parents', friends', and wife's death were part of his working out his faith with fear and trembling as an honest process of living, allowing us evangelically to experience the Last Battle, death, without going out into the darkness, alienated eternally from God, but to come to Jesus, or Aslan's mane, and find comfort there in Heaven.

Another reason why Lewis dissents from any future, eschatological inferences involves his view of Providence and Predestination. For him, *Das macht Nichts*; it does not matter. If it turned out there was no such thing as eternal life, Lewis asks, "Would that be a moment for

---

[32] C. S. Lewis, *The Problem of Pain* (New York: Macmillan Publishing Company, 1978), 125.
[33] C. S. Lewis, *The Problem of Pain*, 125.

changing sides?"[34] The Sovereignty of God is sufficient for Lewis. He would rather emphasize personal evangelical relationships with God through Christ since "personal hopes and fears have to get in first."[35] Thus, justification and salvation are priorities for the Christian; the remainder, including doctrines of eschatology, can be explored later by sanctification. Lewis notes the "Jewish convert tends to stress Christ as king and conqueror; Gentiles more likely start from the priestly sacrificial and intercessory role."[36] Lewis is missing progressive dispensation or areas of biblical history here, separating the Jewish religion theologically from Christianity. He further associates the judgement of Christ with this separation: "Psalmists exhibit an attitude of Jewish confidence, while the Christian trembles because he knows he is a sinner."[37] Was David not recognizing his sin in Psalms? In addition, Lewis creates a divisive picture of judgement: "The Jews cry to God for justice, instead of injustice; the Christians cry to God for mercy instead of justice."[38] What is lacking in Lewis's "Mere Christianity" is a working out of his salvation with fear and trembling, through Old Testament prophecy, through Armageddon, through the Millennial reign of Christ as king, and Christ's ultimate conquering over death, Satan, and all nations. However, Lewis never lessens the importance of Jewish religion, calling Christianity its fulfillment, but also "the fulfillment of what was vaguely hinted at in all religions at their best."[39] Again, Lewis needs to beware a creeping ecumenical pluralism, many religions being treated equally, in his work, especially in *Mere Christianity* where the hallway is the quest for Christianity, not the rooms of the many different religions. Robert Jeffress explores the necessity for no other God but the God of Jesus (*Not All Roads lead to Heaven*). Predestination and Providence for the Jewish people become a "burden as well as a blessing by being chosen."[40] Lewis

---

[34] C. S. Lewis, *Letters to Malcolm,* 120.
[35] C. S. Lewis, *Reflections on Psalms,* 40.
[36] C. S. Lewis, *Reflections on Psalms,* 124.
[37] C. S. Lewis, *Christian Reflections,* 125.
[38] C. S. Lewis, *Reflections on Psalms,* 10.
[39] C. S. Lewis, *God in the Dock,* 54.
[40] C. S. Lewis, *God in the Dock,* 85.

defines "Pre-determinism" as "Pre-determined," since the syllable "pre" lets in "the notion of eternity as simply an older time—but for God, it is the endless present."[41]

Therefore, Lewis hesitates concerning the development of an eschatological or future doctrine for the progressive dispensation eras or evolution of Jesus Christ on biblical grounds. He equates predicting the reign of Jesus, the apocalypse, and the Second Coming of Jesus as foolish predictions of the future. Like a dramatic play, we are merely to play well the scenes and that should "concern us much more than to guess about the scenes that follow it."[42] For Lewis, "Predictions of Jesus seen as being in a class with other apocalyptic writings seem tedious and unedifying to modern tastes."[43] Predictability belongs to science, not to human history; we simply existentially go on doing our duty. However, we are not like Luigi Pirandello's play, "Six Characters in Search of an Author" or Becket's "Waiting for Godot." We have the assurance of the presence of God, not due to imagination, but even when we are desperate for his presence. The rest is left to the "tremendous mystery" in the Mind of Christ, as Dr. W.A. Criswell used to say, *"tremendum mysterion"*. Ultimately, Lewis leaves us with an open-mindedness since "The question of Predestination and Free-will is to my mind undiscussable, insoluble; I suspect it is meaningless."[44] His conclusion to predestination is "the real inter-relation between God's omnipotence and man's freedom is something we can't find out."[45] Lewis leaves us with "an omniscient, all knowing, and providential, omnipresent God whose effects must have been present to Him for all eternity."[46] However, we cannot forsake loving the Lord with all our heart *and mind,* continuing our quest, conforming to the *imago dei,* experiencing the journey of the soul with the "baptism of the imagination."

---

[41] C. S. Lewis, *Letters to Malcolm,* 110.

[42] C. S. Lewis, *The World's Last Night and Other Essays* (New York: Harcourt Brace Jovanovich, 1960), 104.

[43] C. S. Lewis, *The World's Last Night,* 95.

[44] C. S. Lewis, *Letters,* 245-46.

[45] C. S. Lewis, *Letters* (August 3, 1953), 252.

[46] C. S. Lewis, *Letters* (April 6, 1955).

Discovering the Early Works of C. S. Lewis

Boxen (Written circa 1904-1915; Published 1985)

The sea port and the railway station were beginning points for the spiritual journey of C. S. Lewis. He creates with Warnie Animal-Land, including a geographical sketch of countries like India, Poinsee, Dolphinland, and Mouse-Land. Even though these geographical locations are in the imagination, Lewis is careful, including the general revelation of Nature for creatures, for example, in Mouse-Land: "The ancient Mice believed that at sun-set the sun cut a hole in the earth for itself."[47] His infatuation with Creation and science appeals to his imagination at an early age. The maps in his sketchbook are crudely hand drawn although capture the childish creativity of the curious child in a fantasy world being composed. He realizes the contradictions of true science in cartography and latitudes with "…the climates and products of many countries being apparently incompatible with the latitudes to which all maps assign them."[48] Of course, Lewis recognizes the juxtaposition of the imagination with reality and with his own wit ends the whole enterprise of constructing the geography to future readers and scholars:

How far this puzzle could be solved by assuming for the axis of the Boxonian globe an angle different from the terrestrial, is a question which the present writer feels himself incompetent to discuss. He is therefore reluctantly compelled to leave the whole geographical problem to some future Boxonologist.[49]

In the first story in *Boxen*, "The King's Ring," the ring is stolen. One wonders if this idea occurred later to his friendship with J.R.R. Tolkien, in the Lord of the Rings, where the ring is stolen for power of magic. The story ends with King Bunny retrieving his ring. The characters all

---

[47] C. S. Lewis, *Boxen,* edited by Walter Hooper (San Diego: Harcourt Brace, 1985).
[48] C. S. Lewis, *Boxen,* 206.
[49] C. S. Lewis, *Boxen,* 206.

dialog like rugged sailors, the struggle between good and evil in their characters. This moral value system will reoccur throughout the writings of C. S. Lewis in his future essays and literature. The second story, Manx against Manx, entails the motif of the nightmare. The Mouse awakes to find his tail cut off and "mysteriously missing." He thought to himself, "it must have been only a bad nightmare."[50] Later, it is discovered it was the clever setting of a trap for the mouse. The nightmare also becomes the setting for the dream of *Dymer*, Lewis' epic poem as a child. Dreams are an entrance into the world of fantasy and the imagination. In most of the chronology following the tales of Animal-Land, Lewis discusses the succession of Kings, the rebellions between countries and revolutions within countries, capturing the historical development of Kings not only in his own land, but parallel to the Kings and Judges chronicled in the Holy Bible. Enthralled with the magical world of King Arthur, Lewis enters into his own imaginative world of Kings: King Bunny, Bubish, Hacom, King Mouse. He includes Princes and Princesses. The Battles of Porcine war and the Feline revolt are predecessors to Tolkien's great Battle for Middle Earth and the great battle for the kingdom of Narnia. The political struggles and governmental revolutions capture the socialistic, communistic influences in Lewis' own times. The class struggle is imminent between the Commonwealth and the middle class with the rise of the Chessaries. The democratic rising of the commonwealth is overthrown by the dictatorship of the Balkyns. Lewis remarks, "The first horrors of the Russian revolution were still fresh in everyone's mind"[51] when he recollects his childhood. The abolition of slavery is a crowning achievement in Animal-Land with the restoration of the Monarchy. Ultimately, the moral lesson of the tales and history of *Boxen* is for Lewis, "a conversion to good living by fighting."[52] The *Journey of the Tortoise*[53] is the story of a sailor embarking on a journey, discovering good and evil just as the *Voyage of the Dawn Treader* is a journey in the *Chronicles of*

---

[50] C. S. Lewis, *Boxen*, 35.

[51] C. S. Lewis, *Dymer, Preface x*.

[52] C. S. Lewis, *Boxen*, 184.

[53] C. S. Lewis, *Boxen*, 146.

Narnia. We are all converted by the spiritual warfare between good and evil, a struggle with the principalities of evil, by accepting the victorious salvation of Jesus Christ: "For our battle is not against flesh and blood, but against the rulers, against the authorities, against the world powers of this darkness, against the spiritual forces of evil in the heavens" (Ephesians 6:12 HCSB).

Letters to Children (1944, Published 1985)

C. S. Lewis cared for children because he remembered the "common, universally human, ground,"[54] good times and tough times of his own childhood, captured in his work, *Letters to Children*: "Lewis's understanding of children came from another source—it came from within himself. He wrote, 'When I was ten, I read fairy tales in secret and would have been ashamed if I had been found doing so. Now that I am fifty I read them openly. When I became a man, I put away childish things, including the fear of childishness and the desire to be very grown up.'[55] Lewis followed Paul's advice as he grew closer to Christ in his image coming to Him as child (1 Corinthians 13:11 HCSB), but not forsaking his discipleship maturing as a child of God. Lewis never lost the imagination of a child but captures the reality of a real life of joy and suffering on his own spiritual journey. Lewis regrets not feeling the suffering of Christ as a child, not as a duty from adult Sunday school "dragons," but as a revelation from the childhood felt imagination of Christ's suffering.[56] We are made in the image of God, *imago dei*, and Lewis believes his writing began with pictures, images[57], of the dressed

---

[54] Lyle Dorsette and Marjorie Lamp Mead, editors, *C. S. Lewis, Letters to Children* (New York: Macmillan Publishing Company, 1985), Introduction, 6.

[55] C. S. Lewis, "On Three Ways of Writing for Children," *On Stories and Other Essays in Literature,* edited by Walter Hooper (New York: Harcourt Brace, 1982), 42.

[56] C.S. Lewis, *On Stories*, 47.

[57] C.S. Lewis, *On Stories*, 46.

animals in *Boxen* or with the lamppost and creatures in *The Lion, Witch, and the Wardrobe,* a journey from *Boxen to Narnia.*

*Dymer (Published 1926)

From the blissful garden of the imagination, C. S. Lewis the child experiences the worldly Fall after the loss of his mother. His feelings are captured in one of the first works ever written, *Dymer*, when he was forced to attend a public school at age seventeen. Already the kernel and seeds for Lewis' struggle with God as a reluctant convert were being sown in his childhood since by "at least the age of six, I had a romantic longing."[58] Thus, "*Sehnsucht* or the search for God played an unusually central part in my experience."[59] In addition, Lewis reflects upon his public school experience, hatred of the army, hatred of the "new" psychology idolatry of the modern age, and the first horrors of the Russian revolution still fresh on everyone's mind shaping his writing of *Dymer.* Like Dymer, Lewis was destined to struggle between the harsh reality of the world and the world of the fantastic imagination:

By the time I wrote Dymer I had come into a state of angry revolt against that spell of the Christian dream, escaping from illusions of adolescence I exercised about the fantasy of wishful thinking and unmasking the Christian dream that Dymer dreams in that form in the world of fantasy (Canto VII, Dymer).[60]

The images or pictures of Jesus on the cross are clear just as the descriptions of Sigmund Freud's psychological atheism and killing of his father are clear in his poem, *Dymer.* Lewis begins with the mythological description of Norse god, Odin, transforming the experience to the cross of Jesus Christ at the beginning of his epithet of the work:

Nine nights I hung upon the Tree, wounded with the spear as an

---

[58] C. S. Lewis, *Dymer* (London: J.M. Dent Publications. Distributed by Macmillan, 1926), Preface xi.

[59] C. S. Lewis, *Dymer*, xii.

[60] C. S. Lewis, *Dymer*, xi-xii.

offering to Odin, myself sacrificed to myself...*Dymer* is a story about a man who on some mysterious bride begets a monster: which monster, as soon as it has killed its father becomes a god.[61]

In this passage, the influence of the Norse mythology, of the new psychology of Freud, and the Christian background of C. S. Lewis are already shaping his own journey toward the real myth, the true Christianity later in his life. C. S. Lewis reflects about his own spiritual struggle in his life beginning with his childhood, through adolescence, toward maturity, a struggle with Christianity, scientism, materialism, mysticism, the occult, magic, as an Idealist:

I had no fixed principles, except for a vigilant rejection of Christianity, and everything from strict materialism to theosophy could find by turns an entry, I had been, as boys are, temporarily distracted by what was called "The Occult." Yeats believed in magic, no question of symbolism among my serious books—*Rosa Alchemica*, Voltaire, Lucretius.[62]

Lewis was attracted to the mystical fantasy of William Butler Yeats, his gyre whirlwind of metaphysics acquired by automatic handwriting as a member of Madame Blavatsky's Theosophy Society. He was intrigued by Alchemy and Magic, by the Atheism of Voltaire, and by the Atomistic materialism of Lucretius. Dymer concludes with nothing but the void on his quest.

Lewis later calls these flirtations with atheism, humanism, magic, mysticism, and the occult an outcome of his despair and pessimism beginning at six years old since "Dymer was my hero, a man escaping from illusion, and I had no Christian beliefs when I wrote the poem about a man who attempts to suppose the universe is his friend, but realizes it cannot be done by the bribe of a false magician."[63]

Like Freud's *Future of an Illusion*, God was dead for Lewis, and the idealist wish-fulfillment dream leads to a fear-fulfillment dream.[64]

---

[61] C. S. Lewis, *Dymer*, iv.

[62] C. S. Lewis, *Dymer*, xii-xiii.

[63] C. S. Lewis, *Dymer*, xiii-xiv.

[64] Harvey Solganick, *Freud's Search of the Soul: Theories, Translations, and Truths*: Unpublished dissertation (Arlington, Texas: The University of Texas at Arlington, 1998).

Dymer defies the magician who had tempted him and faces his destiny. Ultimately, the death-wish overcomes Dymer and his hope and purpose are cut short when he dies by the spear, realizing "the stars remain and the obedient planets still will spin around the sun."[65] Later, Lewis will recognize the design of the universe by a Designer and will accept natural revelation, but at this point in his life he cannot accept a Sovereign God who can offer him repentance: "I must undo my own sins by the earthly law."[66] Dymer realizes he has lost his Eden; magic is all accursed with demons, alchemy, witches and devils; love will not save him since it is only bodily lust and materialism, a lie of idealistic beauty. Like Lewis, Dymer cries out "Great God, take back your world."[67] Dymer awakes from his idealistic dream. There is no perfect world, created by God or by man's cities with eugenics and social engineering. Only the war remains, the battle living in the waking world that will not end. Dymer's realization, one persistent in Lewis' life also, remains: "Joy slickers on razor's edge of the present and then is gone."[68] Fortunately, Lewis will realize that there is a Creator, a Designer, a natural revelation, but he will also be surprised by a special revelation bringing him a surprise, Joy in Christ.

---

[65] C. S. Lewis, *Dymer,* Canto IX, 88;94.

[66] C. S. Lewis, *Dymer*, Canto VI., 68.

[67] C. S. Lewis, *Dymer*, Canto V, 53.

[68] C. S. Lewis, *Dymer*, Canto V, 51.

Implications for Evangelism and Discipleship

What lessons can we learn from the childhood of C. S. Lewis? How can we apply his life discoveries to a model for evangelism and discipleship?

Parental Guidance, Homeschooling, Practical Vocations, and the Foundation of Religion

1. *Education of the child begins in the environment of the home.* A child should be given the law of the prophets and the good news of the gospel as early as possible by his or her parents as part of homeschooling. Christian values should be applied to the practical life of the child, preparing the child for a vocation. The foundation of religion should begin with Bible reading and study as early as possible.

C. S. Lewis, or "Jack," was reared with strong values in the home. Education begins in the home. Jesus himself was homeschooled by Mary, his mother. Joseph taught Jesus carpentry, a practical application of knowledge. C. S. Lewis expressed both academic ideas but also could supply many practical examples in his works. He was impressed by the railroad workers, the shipyard workers, as well as by the academics in his life. My own father was a shipyard welder in Brooklyn, New York, but desired his son become educated in higher education as well. Like Jesus told his parents when they sought him and found him in the synagogue, teaching the Rabbis, "We must be about my Father's business." Let us look at the homeschooling of Jesus as a background for understanding the significance of "teaching a child in the way he should go."

What was the Education of Jesus like? Belief, Knowledge, or Truth

Alfred Edersheim defines the Rabbinical tradition for teaching: Rabbinism is "outward obedience to the Law and righteousness from works." [69] However, one could not find any Systematic Theology in Rabbinism; only what ideas the Haggadah stated toward God. C. S. Lewis also did not create a systematic theology in his own works. Rabbis

---

[69] Alfred Edersheim, *The Life and Times of Jesus the Messiah* (Henrickson Publishers, 1993), 74-5.

utilized Dialogue—the Angels and Almighty Himself converse with Rabbis and the discussion of Academies, transmitted by the aid of an earthly Rabbi, who is engaged in academic studies. C. S. Lewis engaged in dialogue in his literary works as well as with his audience rhetorically in his essays.

The peril occurs when Replacement of the Law happens—the traditionalism of Rabbinical teachings supersedes the Old Testament. However, the Coming of Jesus completes the Law by the inward spirit. For example, Saul studied with Gamaliel the Rabbi. After Saul's conversion, he calls himself the "chief of sinners and Pharisees":

I thank Christ Jesus our Lord, who has strengthened me, because He considered me faithful, putting me into service, even though I was formerly a blasphemer and a persecutor and a violent aggressor. Yet I was shown mercy because I acted ignorantly in unbelief; and the grace of our Lord was more than abundant, with the faith and love which are found in Christ Jesus. It is a trustworthy statement, deserving full acceptance, that Christ Jesus came into the world to save sinners, among whom I am foremost of all (1 Tim 1:12-15 NAS).

2. The child is prideful and will grow up to be boastful if not taught Christian values of humility and serving others.

C. S. Lewis wrote a Chapter in *Mere Christianity* on "Pride and Competition," indicating the differences between healthy pride and competitive pride. Lewis views pride as a hierarchical sin, from which all other sins derive in his Anglican tradition: "Pride leads to every other vice: it is the complete anti-God state of mind." Certainly, pride comes before the fall, in Lucifer's attempt to usurp the throne and be God, as well as in the Garden of Eden, where Adam and Eve pursue prideful knowledge. However, sin results from the deceitful heart, and begins as a speck growing into obsession as part of our sinful human nature. Pride prevents fellowship with one another as well as with God.

Paul recognized this boasting pride of the Pharisaic Rabbis:

> "The Pharisee stood and was praying this to himself:
> 'God, I thank You that I am not like other people:
> swindlers, unjust, adulterers, or even like this tax
> collector." (Luke 18:11 NAS) But a Pharisee named
> Gamaliel, a teacher of the Law, respected by all the
> people, stood up in the Council and gave orders to
> put the men outside for a brief time (Acts 5:34 NAS).
> But perceiving that one group were Sadducees and the
> other Pharisees, Paul began crying out in the Council,
> "Brethren, I am a Pharisee, a son of Pharisees; I am on
> trial for the hope and resurrection of the dead!" (Acts
> 23:6 NAS)

> ...since they have known about me for a long time,
> if they are willing to testify, that I lived as a Pharisee
> according to the strictest sect of our religion. (Acts
> 26:5 NAS)

> ...circumcised the eighth day, of the nation of Israel, of
> the tribe of Benjamin, a Hebrew of Hebrews; as to the
> Law, a Pharisee (Philippians 3:5 NAS).

3. *Teach the child the way of studying Christianity, reading the Bible, offering the gospel to others, and maturing with discipleship in sound doctrine.*

Jesus learned the educational method of the Rabbis: Questioning through Rhetorical questions, Riddles, and Puzzles; The Art of Narrative through moral stories and fables, unfinished narratives, parables; Recitation of Dogma of the Torah law, Haggadah Rabbinical Sayings, Rabbinical authority. C. S. Lewis uses all these rhetorical devices in his literature, essays, fantasies, stories, science-fiction, apologetic treatises. The Teaching of Jesus is founded upon asking the right questions and learning the answers by inquiry, by what Randy Newman calls

"Questioning Evangelism."[70] Thus, Jesus utilizes Parables[71] and Recitation of Old Testament Scripture throughout the Bible.

4. The child should learn no separation between knowledge and wisdom, including academic preparation as well as vocational preparation, as serving the Lord in everything the child says and does.

The Education of Jesus included Apprenticeship and Vocation.[72] He was taught Hebrew language and law in the home and by the Rabbi Teachers, but his father, Joseph, taught him carpentry as an apprentice and model for his practical life. Jesus underwent Biblical Child Development[73] as fully human in these phases of human growth, while being fully divine in his spiritual growth:

a. The newborn babe (Isa. 9:6)
b. The suckling (Isa. 11: 8)
c. The suckling asking for food (Lam. 4:4)
d. The weaned child (Isa.28:9)
e. The child clinging to the mother (Jer. 40:7)
f. The child becomes free firmly (from the roots to the Branch)

5. In the home, the child learns the art of Christian role and responsibility built upon love and views the model of relationship between husband and wife, siblings, and neighbors as good will.

The law written upon the heart is learned from obedience to parents:

---

[70] Randy Newman, *Questioning Evangelism: Engaging People's Hearts the Way Jesus did* (Grand Rapids, MI: Kregel, 2004).
Newman addresses questions such as:
* Why are Christians so intolerant?
* To why does a good God allow evil and suffering?
* Why should anyone worship a God who allowed 9/11?
* Why should we believe an ancient book written by dead Jewish males?
* If Jesus is so great, why are some of his followers such jerks?
[71] Steve Smith, *Dying to Preach: Embracing the Cross in the Pulpit* (Grand Rapids, MI: Kregel, 2009).
Smith demonstrates the use of parables and narrative in the teachings of Jesus.
[72] Josh McDowell, *More than a Carpenter* (Tyndale House Publishers, 2009).
[73] Edersheim, 154.

loving care is the mother's role; the father's role in the home is the worship leader.

The first education experienced by the child is the mother's example (Proverbs Woman/Jewish women of New Testament). The mother prepared the Sabbath meal; lit the candles; cleaned the unleavened bread. The Mezuzah blessed the home to honor the Lord (Psalm 121:8).

The second education is the father's teaching knowledge of the Torah when the child learned to speak: liturgy, Bible, short prayers, selections from sages, the culture of memory and recitation. Hymns were taught by Psalms and the Hillel (Psalms 113-118). Notice, Jesus continued in respectful obedience to his parents' love and education for him in the home:

His mother said to Him, "Son, why have You treated us this way? Behold, your father and I have been anxiously looking for You." 49 And He said to them, "Why is it that you were looking for Me? Did you not know that I had to be in My Father's house?"50 But they did not understand the statement which He had made to them. 51 And He went down with them and came to Nazareth, and He continued in subjection to them; and His mother treasured all these things in her heart. (Luke 2: 48-51)

6. *The child should be provided a schooling not only private or public, but also a biblical schooling from the church, including sound doctrine throughout the formative years of the child in a planned curriculum.*

By the fifth or sixth year, every child was sent to school based upon previous home schooling. The child learned the alphabet and writing to advance to Rabbinical schools or Academies with a moral and religious goal as the ultimate goal. From open air schools developed schools in the Synagogues; students and teacher sat in a semicircle on the floor. The teacher was the Chazzan or officer of the Synagogue.

Reading the Bible, for up to ten years, the texts were the books of Leviticus, the Pentateuch, and the Prophets in the Bible; ten to fifteen, the Mishnah or traditional law; after that age, theological discussions over the Talmud occurred in the Academies of the Rabbis. Jesus then knew the Laws of Leviticus, the Laws of Moses, and the Prophets, and would ask "Have you not read?" reciting the Old Testament in His own teachings. (Luke 4:16) Note that the gospel was the evangelical center of his education, preparing Jesus to spread the good news:

> And Jesus returned to Galilee in the power of the Spirit, and news about Him spread through all the surrounding district. And He began teaching in their synagogues and was praised by all. And He came to Nazareth, where He had been brought up; and as was His custom, He entered the synagogue on the Sabbath, and stood up to read. And the book of the prophet Isaiah was handed to Him. And He opened the book and found the place where it was written, "THE SPIRIT OF THE LORD IS UPON ME, BECAUSE HE ANOINTED ME TO PREACH THE GOSPEL TO THE POOR. HE HAS SENT ME TO PROCLAIM RELEASE TO THE CAPTIVES, AND RECOVERY OF SIGHT TO THE BLIND, TO SET FREE THOSE WHO ARE OPPRESSED, TO PROCLAIM THE FAVORABLE YEAR OF THE LORD." And He closed the book, gave it back to the attendant and sat down; and the eyes of all in the synagogue were fixed on Him. And He began to say to them, "Today this Scripture has been fulfilled in your hearing." (Luke 4:14-21)

Thus, the child will continue to grow and become strong, increasing in wisdom and like Jesus, the grace of God was upon be upon him (Luke 2:40 NAS). Notice the method (listening, questioning, understanding, wisdom) and the content (God's Word and law, statutes) because of discipleship training of the child, creating spiritual character (stature):

> Then, after three days they found Him in the temple, sitting amid the teachers, both listening to them and asking them questions. 47 And all who heard Him were

amazed at His understanding and His answers. (Luke 2:46 NAS)

And Jesus kept increasing in wisdom and stature, and in favor with God and men (Luke 2:50 NAS).

Jesus achieved, like a Christian child, Knowledge, Belief, Truth, Wisdom,[74] demonstrating the model for discipleship education: How do we know what we know?[75] He accomplished this, by Questioning and Doubt; Belief, opinion and Faith; Truth and Revelation; Wisdom and Application; Intellectual Virtue and Moral Virtue.

---

[74] Harvey Solganick, *Creative, Constructive, Critical Thinking for the Christian* (Arlington, TX: London Press, 2013).
[75] Robert Jeffress, *How can I know? Answers to Life's Seven most important Questions* (Nashville, TN: Worthy Books, 2013).

CHAPTER 2

Youth, Discipleship, Discipline, Education

Introduction: The Hard Knock from Emotions to Apologetics

Born Clive Staples Lewis on November 29, 1898 in Belfast, Northern Ireland, to Albert James Lewis (1863-1929) and Flora Augusta Hamilton Lewis (1862-1908), Lewis always looked up to his brother, Warren Hamilton Lewis, who had been born on June 16, 1895. In 1905 the Lewis family moved to their new home, "Little Lea," on the outskirts of Belfast, where he shared an imaginative childhood with his brother and the love of his mother and father. However, in 1908 his mother died of cancer on August 23, Albert Lewis' (her husband's) birthday. At the wishes of his father, C. S. Lewis (nicknamed "Jack") and Warren (nicknamed "Warnie") were sent to Wynyard School in England, a grammar school where discipline was taught in a strict curriculum. Then in 1910, Lewis attended Campbell College, Belfast for one term due to serious respiratory difficulties. Continuing his education, Lewis, from 1911-1913, studied at Cherbourg School, Malvern England, following Warnie, remaining remarkably poor in mathematics, unlike his mother, but evidencing an increasing affection for *"Northernness"* (e.g. Wagner's music and Norse mythology). It was during this time that he abandoned his childhood Christian faith.

This refutation of his faith led him to his studies from 1914-1916 with W.T. Kirkpatrick, "The Hard Knock," called by his students. Here he was exposed to extensive literary and philosophical studies (Latin, Greek, French, German, and Italian) under the private tuition of W. T. Kirkpatrick ("The Great Knock").

The Hard Knock Kirkpatrick: The Roots of Apologetics

"A man can't be always defending the truth;
there must be a time to feed on it."

... C. S. Lewis. *Reflections on the Psalms.*

"The riddles of God are more satisfying than the solutions of man."
... G.K. Chesterton. *The Everlasting Man*. Ignatius, 2000.

Following in the footsteps of C. S. Lewis's education, while reforming my faith, accepting Christ, against the "hard knock" of agnosticism, humanism, mysticism, and atheism, I noticed a perilous, parallel philosophical journey taken by C. S. Lewis in response to his own battle with his Christian walk. Lewis constantly retained an admiring endearment to his teacher, W. T. Kirkpatrick, or as Lewis calls him, "The Great Knock." Like Lewis, I also admired my atheistic and agnostic philosophers and teachers during my higher education for their logical rationality and their pervasive intellect. Like Lewis, I also read such atheistic thinkers like Bertrand Russell (*A Free Man's Worship; Why I am not a Christian*), Paul Kurtz (*A Humanist Manifesto*), Kai Nelson (*Ethics without God*), Sigmund Freud (*The Future of an Illusion*), Karl Marx (*Das Kapitel*), Friedrich Nietzsche (*Human, All too Human*), and B.F. Skinner (*Beyond Freedom and Dignity*). I even attended a debate at The University of Texas, Austin, between atheist Madeline O'Hare and a Unitarian minister. I was influenced by my philosophy professors, Dr. Robert Solomon's existential humanism as we talked over coffee at Les Amis Café at The University of Texas at Austin and was consoled during the death of my mother while attending North Texas State University by Richard M. Owsley's existential phenomenology (I called him, "The Wise Owl of Minerva"). In my literary background, I studied postmodern deconstruction with Dr. Victor Vitanza at The University of Texas at Arlington. From my journey of past darkness into the present light of Jesus Christ, I realize now that these educational experiences and personal encounters make me stronger in defending the Christian faith, just as C. S. Lewis's examination of his childhood Christianity through agnosticism and atheism sharpens his apologetic skills. Apologetics concerns defending the faith, but one must have the faith first as a foundation to defend it. Apologetics without evangelicalism and discipleship is dead.

The development of an apologetic against agnosticism and atheism is the outcome of being saved by questioning evangelism and discipleship study, an interpersonal relational evangelism based upon the friendship relationship between W.T. Kirkpatrick and C. S. Lewis. A.N. Wilson, in *C. S. Lewis: A Biography*, calls W.T. Kirkpatrick, "a valued teacher and friend" to Lewis[76]. C. S. Lewis calls W.T. Kirkpatrick, "a hard, satirical atheist who taught me to think"[77]. Baylor University professor, Robert C. Wood, captures this philosophical method of Lewis: "From his early tutelage under the atheist rationalist, W.T. Kirkpatrick, Lewis had learned to relish dialectic, the cut and thrust of intellectual repartee"[78]. In *Surprised by Joy*, Lewis writes, "My debt to him [Kirkpatrick] is very great, my reverence to this day undiminished"[79]. In their personal, Platonic relationship, Lewis writes, "Here was a man who thought not about you but about what you said"[80]. In *Surprised by Joy*, reflecting Kirkpatrick's influence, Lewis writes, "I maintained that God did not

---

[76] A.N. Wilson, *C. S. Lewis: A Biography* (New York: W. W. Norton, 2002), 171.

[77] C. S. Lewis, *Miracles: How God intervenes in Nature and Human Affairs* (New York: Macmillan, 1940).

[78] Robert C. Wood, "Conflict and Convergence on Fundamental Matters in C. S. Lewis and J.R.R. Tolkien" (Published in *Renascence*, 15 October 2005). <http://www3.baylor.edu/~Ralph_Wood/lewis/L ewisTolkienTension.pdf>

[79] C. S. Lewis, *Surprised by Joy* (Harvest Books, 1966), 148.

[80] C. S. Lewis, *Surprised by Joy*, 137.

exist. I was also very angry with God for not existing. I was equally angry with Him for creating a world" [81].

Another inspirational author, G.K. Chesterton, also influenced C. S. Lewis' agnostic journey: "The riddles of God are more satisfying than the solutions of man"[82]. From this model of a Platonic, intellectual relationship between friends, an apologetic, based upon relational, fideism, evidential, presuppositional, and cumulative approaches, becomes essential for defending the Christian faith against agnosticism and atheism experienced by C. S. Lewis in his life and works. The outcome demonstrates even God can work in mysterious ways through atheism to strengthen the Christian faith, so, as Jesus reminds us, "Listen! I stand at the door and knock. If anyone hears My voice and opens the door, I will come in to him and have dinner with him, and he with Me" (Revelation 3:20 HCSB). Otherwise, the consequences of not believing are detrimental: "Then you will stand outside and knock on the door, saying, 'Lord, open up for us!' He will answer you, 'I don't know you or where you're from'" (Luke 13:25 HCSB).

C. S. Lewis wavered in his Christian faith several times, hardening his heart and mind toward God. As a child, the death of his mother affected him severely. Again, as a young adult, Lewis buried God in the battlefield, waging his own battle for and against God. Lewis himself said, "The early loss of my mother, great unhappiness at school, and the shadow of the last war and presently the experience of it, had given me a very pessimistic view of existence. My atheism was based on it"[83]. Finally, as an older man, Lewis was stricken by the death of his wife, Joy Davidman, and reconstituted his faith in God after a period of confusing despair. However, all these psycho-biographical and psycho-historical experiences also made Lewis into a stronger man of faith. As a child, he "put away childish things;" as a young adult, he dedicated himself on the

---

[81] C. S. Lewis, Surprised by Joy, 115.

[82] G. K. Chesterton, *The Everlasting Man* (Ignatius, 2000).

[83] Nicholi Armani, *The Question of God: School Days. PBS documentary* (4 November 2005).
http://www.pbs.org/wgbh/questionofgod/transcript/school.html.

battlefield to the "glory of God;" and as an older, mature Christian, after "many trials and tribulations," he was drawn closer (what Lewis calls *Sehnsucht*) to God through his "mere Christianity." Thus, all the road before him, his journey, was not only a personal growth in Christianity, but also an apologetic model for defending the faith against agnosticism and atheism, for himself, but also for others.

First, a definition of some terms would help the reader grasp Lewis' spiritual struggle. According to Anthony C. Thiselton, in *A Concise Encyclopedia of the Philosophy of Religion*, "Atheism denotes the denial of the existence of God, to be distinguished from Agnosticism, the belief that to know whether or not God exists is impossible"[84]. Although many proclaim Lewis as an atheist at times in his life, I believe, from a Protestant perspective, he maintained his faith and matured in his Christianity. However, periods of agnosticism haunted him. It is my contention that Lewis never lost his faith but grew stronger through his tests and trials of his faith. His faith was shaken emotionally based upon a fideism apologetic belief in God, but he never believed in a purely evidentialist claim for God's existence, and ultimately, never gives up his classical, rational apologetic approach for understanding his faith. In other words, he did not have enough faith to remain an atheist. At least five distinct approaches to apologetics have guided most seekers: 1) The Classical Method/ Presuppositional method utilizes deductive logic and philosophical rationalism for constructive argumentation, examining and disclosing premises and presuppositions. Thus, reason justifies faith. 2) Evidentialist Apologetics emphasizes empirical evidence, verification with science, archeology, factual history, etc. 3) Reformed Apologetics offers a regenerative spirit, based upon biblical standards, theological doctrines of predestination, Christianity versus false science. 4) Fideism Apologetics calls us to obey the Truth of a personal theology, with faith beyond science, revelation beyond history, based upon inspiration and experience. 5) Cumulative Case Method insists all methods are utilized to achieve the Truth, including classical arguments: theism; personal

---

[84] Anthony C. Thiselton, *A Concise Encyclopedia of the Philosophy of Religion* (Grand Rapids: Baker Academic Books, 2002), 18.

experience and moral behavior (Fideism); the role of the Holy Spirit in revealed truth (Reformed); evidence for beliefs (Evidentialist)[85]. Lewis, as a "reluctant convert," probably became a cumulative case apologist, building his faith, searching for the existence of God in his life. At times, Lewis would even turn to mysticism as a phase for his agnostic inquiry, but this phase could not last for the master apologist. According to David C. Downing, "Ultimately, the contemporary trend in world mysticism must be found wanting, both for its logical inconsistencies and for its empty promise of *gnōsis* without *kenōsis*, the gaining of knowledge without the losing of self"[86]. Ultimately, Lewis gains both the knowledge of being a Christian and the loss of the old creature, becoming the new creature in Christ.

How exactly did W.T. Kirkpatrick's atheism influence Lewis? Why did atheists, like Freud, Marx, Nietzsche, Russell, reject God eventually, while Lewis accepted the Lord?[87] I have always been intrigued by my Jewish background why great thinkers reject Christianity as I did for years. For example, Sigmund Freud was interested in God's existence

---

[85] Steven B. Cowan, editor, *Five Views on Apologetics* (Grand Rapids: Zondervan, 2000). William Lane Craig presents the Classical method. Gary R. Habermas presents the Evidential Method. Paul D. Feinberg presents the Cumulative Case Method. John M. Frame presents the Presuppositional Method. Kelly James Clark represents the Reformed Epistemological Method. [See Solganick, Harvey. "Apologetics Worldviews," *Encyclopedia of Christian Civilization* (Blackwell, 2012).]

[86] David C. Dowling, *Mysticism in C. S. Lewis: Into the Region of Awe* (Downers Grove, IL: InterVarsity Press, 2005), 148.

[87] Kurt Baier, *Problems of Life and Death: A Humanist Perspective* (New York: Prometheus Books, 1997).

Sigmund Freud, *The Future of an Illusion*. (W. W. Norton, 1989).

Paul Kurtz, A *Humanist Manifesto One and Two* (New York: Prometheus, 1973).

Karl Marx, *Das Kapital* (Gateway, 1999).

Kai Nelson, *Ethics without God* (New York: Prometheus, 1990).

Friedrich Nietzsche, *Human, All too Human* (Cambridge: Cambridge UP, 1996).

Bertrand Russell, *A Free Man's Worship* (Mosher, 1927).

Bertrand Russell, *Why I am not a Christian.* (Touchstone, 1967).

Skinner, B. F. *Beyond Freedom and Dignity.* (Indianapolis: Hackett, 2002).

before he wrote *Future of an Illusion*, and he asked his best friend, Oskar Pfister, a Lutheran minister, who this God, Jesus, was. Pfister did not want to discuss Jesus with Freud but was more concerned with psychological programs in the Church.[88] The difference in Lewis was his intellectual approach combined with his personal relationships. Friendship models, like W.T. Kirkpatrick and Owen Barfield, influenced his intrigue with atheism, while other models, like C.K. Chesterton and J.R. Tolkien, inspired his Christianity. For example, Owen Barfield attempted to derive a philosophy based upon *Anthropos* or human nature alone[89]. Let us examine the life and teaching style of W.T. Kirkpatrick as it influenced C. S. Lewis.

William T. Kirkpatrick (1848-1921), a retired headmaster of Lurgan College, Northern Ireland, served as Lewis's tutor during the years 1914-1917. He was a friend of Lewis' father, Albert Lewis, who had himself been tutored by Kirkpatrick from 1877-1879. When Jack Lewis went to boarding school, he failed miserably, and returned to individualized tutoring, living with Kirkpatrick. Oddly enough, as predestined knowledge by a Presbyterian, Kirkpatrick told Lewis' father, "You may make a writer or a scholar out of him, but you'll not make anything else"[90]. Kirkpatrick used the Socratic method of teaching, making Lewis think through every experience: "If Jack would look outdoors and comment that it was a nice day, Kirkpatrick would vigorously call out "Stop!" and require Jack to define a nice day and explain his reasons for labeling this particular day a nice one"[91]. This logical positivist approach, applying philosophy and linguistics, allowed Lewis to enter

---

[88] Harvey Solganick, *Theories, Translations, and Truths: Freud's Search for the Soul.* Dissertation (Arlington, TX: The University of Texas, 1998). I had been intrigued why a Jewish atheist like myself had become a Christian, while others had not. I studied the letters of Freud in London and Vienna and the Bible he read at the Freud Museum.

[89] Owen Barfield, The Case for Anthroposophy, In *The Barfield Reader,* edited by G. B. Tennyson (Wesleyan University Press, 1999), 151-52.

[90] C. S. Lewis, *Surprised by Joy.* (New York: Harvest Books, 1966), 183.

[91] Marvin D. Hinton and Bruce L. Edwards, "William T. Kirkpatrick," In *The C. S. Lewis Reader's Encyclopedia.* (Grand Rapids: Zondervan, 1998), 229.

into a dialectical dialogue with his teacher, whom he called a "purely logical entity," "a Rationalist of the old, high and dry, nineteenth-century type"[92], a style Lewis utilized, as well as wrote about himself in *Surprised by Joy*; as the skeptical, rationalistic MacPhee in *That Hideous Strength*; and as Professor Kirke claims, "What are these schools teaching nowadays!" in *The Chronicles of Narnia*. Professor Kirke in *The Lion, the Witch, and the Wardrobe*, is perhaps patterned after Kirkpatrick[93]. Like Lewis, Kirkpatrick was an eccentric, who wore his best clothes gardening on Sundays than for weekday gardening, rebelling against his strict, traditional Presbyterian upbringing. Kirkpatrick not only insisted that Lewis learn French, German, Italian, Greek, and Latin on his own, but would read original literary selections in the original language, such as *Medea* and Dante's *Divine Comedy*. Thus, Kirkpatrick framed Lewis' whole career and interests as a medieval scholar, linguist, and rational philosopher. Even though he admired the intellectual abilities of Kirkpatrick, the atheistic worldview served as a foil, a dialectical counterargument, for Lewis as he struggled with his own faith: "From him [Kirkpatrick] I learned something about the honor of the intellect and the shame of voluntary inconsistency."[94]

Lewis wrote a letter to Owen Barfield (January 18, 1927) about his battle for God:

> I was thinking about imagination and intellect and the unholy muddle I am in about them at present: undigested scraps of anthroposophy and psychoanalysis jostling with orthodox idealism over a background of good old Kirkian rationalism. Lord what a mess! And all the time (with me) there's the danger of falling back into most childish superstitions, or of running into dogmatic materialism to escape them.[95]

---

[92] C. S. Lewis, *Surprised by Joy,* (New York: Harvest Books, 1966), 139.

[93] Martha Sammons, *Guide through Narnia* (Harold Shaw Publications, 1979), 89.

[94] C. S. Lewis, *Surprised by Joy (New York:* Harvest Books, 1966), 173.

[95] Walter Hooper, editor, Foreword by Owen Barfield, *All my Road before Me: The Diary of C. S. Lewis 1922-1927* (San Diego: Harcourt Brace, 1991), xi.

This dogmatic materialism or atheism was identified with the "Kirkian rationalism" of W.T. Kirkpatrick, and his "childish superstitions" concerned his belief in magic, mysticism, and pseudo-mythology. For C. S. Lewis, Christianity won the battle over atheistic materialism, mysticism, and magic since Christianity was the "real" myth, based on reality after he demythologized all his other beliefs. Lewis had developed an apologetic against atheism.

Atheism, Agnosticism and Anglicanism

What should a Lewis apologetic against atheism look like? Several apologists have offered formal apologetic arguments against atheism.[96] If we apply what C. S. Lewis learned from W.T. Kirkpatrick in his own journey against agnosticism and atheism, we can apply the following precepts:

"He never attacked religion in my presence"[97].

"Here was a man who thought not about you but about what you said"[98].

"My debt to him is very great, my reverence to this day undiminished"[99].

"He was a hard, satirical atheist and the man who taught me to think"[100].

By all means, do not grow weary and give up defending the faith. As an atheist, Kirkpatrick was described by a student as one whose "pistol never missed fire; but he gave you the impression that, if it did, you would be knocked down by the butt-end"[101]. The Lewis family loved W.T. Kirkpatrick, in spite of his atheistic humanism, even until his death on March 22, 1921[102]. In conclusion, the biblical principle of apologetics

---

[96] William Lane Craig and Walter Sinnott-Armstrong, *God: A Debate between a Christian and an Atheist* (Oxford: Oxford UP, 2004).

Norman L. Geisler and Frank Turek, *I don't have enough Faith to be an Atheist.* (Wheaton: Crossway, 2004).

Nicholi, Armani, *The Question of God: C. S. Lewis and Sigmund Freud Debate God, Love, Sex, and the Meaning of Life* (New York: Free Press, 2002).

[97] C. S. Lewis, *Surprised by Joy* (New York: Harvest Books, 1966), 140.

[98] C. S. Lewis, *Surprised by Joy*, 137.

[99] C. S. Lewis, *Surprised by Joy*, 148.

[100] C. S. Lewis, *Miracles* (New York: Macmillan, 1940), 69.

[101] C. S. Lewis, *The Collected Letters of C. S. Lewis, Vol.1: Family Letters, 1905-1931.* (Harper Collins, 2004), I-3.

[102] C. S. Lewis, *The Collected Letters of C. S. Lewis, Vol.1: Family Letters, 1905-1931.* (Harper Collins, 2004), I-1005.

still is the best classical definition of how to do Lewis's apologetics when respectfully encountering a "hard knock" from the atheist:

> "Do not fear what they fear or be disturbed but set apart the Messiah as Lord in your hearts, and always be ready to give a defense to anyone who asks you for a reason for the hope that is in you. However, do this with gentleness and respect, keeping your conscience clear, so that when you are accused, those who denounce your Christian life will be put to shame." (1 Peter 3:14-16 HCSB)

It is a shame that W.T. Kirkpatrick was such an influence on C. S. Lewis by his teaching style and intellectual abilities, but the "hard knock," Kirk, never answered the knock at the door, opening his heart, mind, and soul to the Lord: "'Lord, open up for us!' He will answer you, 'I don't know you or where you're from'" (Luke 13:25 HCSB). Instead, Kirkpatrick was influenced by the depressed philosophies of Bertrand Russell's *Free Man's Worship* and of Schopenhauer's *World as Will*. However, we do know the faith of C. S. Lewis and from whence he came -- out of the darkened despair of the shadowlands of atheism, into the light of the Lord. Lewis' childhood built a foundation for faith by studying the creeds and doctrines of Anglicanism, but he needed a personal relationship with Christ with special revelation through the evangelism of his friends and Joy Davidman to complete his journey of faith into the light of the Lord.

Education: The Roots of Discipleship

C. S. Lewis progressed from agnosticism, mysticism, and atheism to Theism, then ultimately to Christianity by growing in his intellectual understanding of Christianity and the creeds and doctrines of the Anglican church, but he needed another education: life experience and biblical teaching, growing and maturing in the Word of Christ, the "hard knocks" of suffering, all would lead him to a true test of his faith. Not only are we to follow the great commission: "Go you therefore and spread the gospel to the uttermost," but we also need to grow in discipleship. Often, the second half of the great commission is not stressed, "Making disciples of every nation." That includes us. We are thankful to be evangelized and for the revelation of God's Word to us in our salvation, but we must educate ourselves continually in God's Word. As a member of the faculty at Southwestern Seminary, I participated in developing a six year curriculum for discipleship for youth to disciple new Christians.[103] Lewis undergoes five areas of discipleship in his own life: Learning the creeds and doctrines of Christianity through the Anglican Church; testing his faith with agnosticism and atheism; and testing his faith through mysticism and Theosophy; building his rational faith through Theism; and ultimately, experiencing the special revelation of his faith through Christ's suffering on the cross.

---

[103] Harvey Solganick, *Disciple6: Christianity*, Online, edited by Richard Ross, Southwestern Baptist Theological Seminary (Fort Worth, TX: Seminary Hill Press, 2016).

The New Age: Mysticism and Theosophy

Fleeting Fantasies of Magic, Mysticism and Myth

Interrupting his quest for Christianity, Lewis became engaged in magic, mysticism, and myth by dialoguing with his friends at Oxford and Cambridge. Owen Barfield and Charles Williams intrigued him with his emphasis upon Anthroposophy and the writings of Rudolf Steiner and Madame Blavatsky. The Old Age pagan myths including Norse Mythology and Celtic traditions became a New Age concern for Lewis, just as the New Age philosophical worldviews became popular in my search for the soul. Allow me to take a leaf out of the pages of my own soul journey, experiencing the "power points," places of mystical, magic, and mythological insights, as I journeyed through England's Glastonbury and Ireland's Celtic Hebrides regions.

"This land is your land...It belongs to you and me!"---Woody Guthrie

People look at landscapes for signs of a belief system which reciprocates by signifying a meaning for their life's journey. Jack and Warnie shared a magical garden spot in their boyhood imagination, creating a fantasy of Animal Land. Special land areas are designated as "power spots," creating an intentionality of the human consciousness to open itself to extraordinary phenomenal experiences. However, these power spots constitute also an ordinary reality response, pragmatic or practical in praxis, by others. The same form or structure of the land objects create a juxtaposition of phenomena/praxis response, depending upon the responder to the ecological topology or geographical shape of the land. My study[104] of several power spots I experienced in England and Ireland will explore the analogical relationship between the geological shape (morphology) of power spots and the people who perceive and

---

[104] Harvey Solganick, "Phenomenal Power Spots," Presentation in Huma 5303: The New Ethnography.
(Arlington, TX: University of Texas at Arlington, June 30,1994).

create possible significations from them, notably perceived through their perceptions. The techniques of structuralism, postmodernism, and analogical interpretation, emphasized during a Humanities seminar in June 1994, on the "New Ethnology" at the University of Texas at Arlington with Dr. Joseph W. Bastien, influenced my approach to this study. [105] Some of these possible interpretations reflect the presuppositions of Christian and Celtic myths since many of the power spots are in "sacred" sites of England and Scotland. In addition, the philosophies of Paganism, Animism, Pantheism, and Vitalism will serve as relativistic, functional reference points for the pluralistic, possible interpretations by responders in the phenomenological event, the interaction between subject and object.[106] Structural similarities between the Goddess, the Lady, and Mother Nature are unveiled as dialectical positions to the patriarch myths of Creationism and empirical Darwinism as static models.[107] Lewis studied creation myths and opposed reduction materialism in his work against Darwinism, *The Abolition of Man*. Specific target objectifications of the land sites will be limited to those actually visited by the writer in England and Scotland, although some comparative power spots in America are mentioned for clarification.

First, a definition of a "power spot" can be discovered on what is called geographically and psychologically as a "leyline." A "leyline" can be defined as follows:

> It is a straight-line flow of natural energy of a geomagnetic
> or etheric kind, often directional according to season
> or moon phase, which the ancients learned to mark
> out. It is an exact alignment of points. It is part of an
> energy network of nodes and lines which makes up an

---

[105] Joseph W. Bastien, *Mountain of the Condor: Metaphor and Ritual in Andean Allyu* (St. Paul: West, 1978).

[106] Virginia Dominquez, *People as Subject; People as Object* (Madison: University of Wisconsin Press, 1989).

[107] Dominquez's study of significant markers, Israeli celebrations, and collective consciousness influenced my existential, phenomenological approach of a postmodern ethnography.

integral system, the full meaning of which we do not yet understand. Some alignments have been found to relate to the rising or setting points of sun, moon, planets and stars, while others have distinctly topographical significance and yet others have some sort of human-derived meaning.[108]

Thus, a "power spot" is an energy center upon certain points or spots along a leyline:

An energy center or power point is a place where a certain power, timelessness, life-energy and naturalness prevail, where a visitor can change consciousness or shift the context of his or her life perception easily. It is a place which is a hilltop or remarkable feature, or the site of a standing stone, mound, hedge, camp, church or cross or crossroad, aligned to other such points or at the crossing point of leys. It is a place where there have been noteworthy paranormal occurrences, mythological events or old gatherings, festivals, healings or rites. It is a place where there are geomagnetic or geological anomalies or faulting, quartz deposits or unusual topographical features. It is a place where underground

---

[108] [107] Claude Levi-Strauss. *Tristes Tropiques: Sad Tropics.* (New York: Antheum, 1974).

The structural approach by Levi-Strauss and his reaction against static models influenced my approach for possible interpretations of myths and legends on my own journey. A dialogical state exists between the subject, the "I", and the objectified ritual, the "It," which becomes transfigured into the "other," the "thou." The objects are transvalued into human interpretation who in turn transvalue interpretations upon the object. (Martin Buber, *I and Thou* (New York: Scribner's Press); Friedrich Nietzsche, *Beyond Good and Evil* (New York: New American Library).

water flows and where often the ancients installed a
stone or moved the earth.[109]

A power spot, occurring at a space-time event moment,
is then a dynamic interaction between observer and the
observed. The form of the land elicits interpretations
beyond "eidetic meaning" or fantasy of the imagination
in the consciousness of the subject by his or her "lived-
body experience."[110] Lewis read George MacDonald's
Phantases and was influenced in his own development of
"baptism by imagination." Thus, the aesthetic object, in
this case the power spot of the landscape, is completed
only in the consciousness of the present spectator.[111]
The process includes perceptual experience, presence,
representation, imagination, and reflection. The subject
and object are reconciled into the depths of an expressed

---

[109] Palden Jenkins. *Planetary Paths: Energy Centres, ancient remains, leylines, coast and islands*
(Glastonbury, England: Helios Books, 1983).

[110] Maurice Merleau-Ponty, *Phenomenology of Perception* (Paris: Gallimard, 1945).

[111] Mikel Dufrenne, *The Phenomenology of Aesthetic Experience* (Evanston: Northwestern
University Press, 1973).

Both Merleau-Ponty and Dufrenne, French phenomenologists, create a methodology
for approaching the interpretation of the object, not based upon the object or
the subject alone, but by the interrelation or nexus between the two, creating a
"lived-body experience" interpretation, not an aesthetic study of the object itself,
but an interpretation dependent upon the "eidetic reduction" to a grasping of
consciousness as essence. [Edmund Husserl, *Ideas (Ideen)*] Heidegger allows Being
(*Dasein*) to unveil itself to the existential self, giving standing (*Standigkeit*) to both
the consciousness of being (*Bewusstein*) itself, including human consciousness and
Nature itself having its ground in metaphysical consciousness. (Martin Heidegger,
Language, Truth, and Meaning; The Way Back to Metaphysics.)

world.[112] Nature speaks to us as if the object willed itself into its and our existence. All meaning is given in the sensuous, ontological, and cosmological unity of the extraordinary phenomenological event--the power spot occurring on the leyline of our standing space/ time event.[113]

The most focused power spot seems to be Stonehenge in Great Britain. Lewis visited these structures. Here the tourists come to marvel at the structure whose stones are arranged in a circle with other enormous stones placed upon pillars. Conjecture from Celtic and Druid legends states this sacred site was used for sacrifices to the gods for agricultural fertility of the land.[114] Others label it an astronomical center for predicting the phases of the sun and moon. Both phenomena/praxis interpretations could be combined as revitalizing the planting season during the right

---

[112] Carlos Castaneda, *The Fire Within* (New York: Simon and Schuster, 1984). Castaneda views leylines and power spots as "emanations for alignment": "The next truth is that perception takes place because there is in each of us an agent called the assemblage point that selects internal and external emanations for alignment."

[113] Mikel Dufrenne, *The Notion of the A Priori* (Evanston, IL: University of Northwestern Press, 1966). In rather obtuse language, Dufrenne describes the process as "the object in-itself-for-itself, but also in-itself-for-itself-for-us." Both Dufrenne, Merleau-Ponty, and Sartre use French language as the embodiment of a "French tease" when it comes to translating into English their complex French conceptual language. Carlos Castaneda describes it more simply for simpletons as an "extraordinary experience," a "crack between the worlds": "The particular thing to learn is how to get to the crack between the worlds and how to enter the other world...There is a place where the two worlds overlap." (Carlos Castaneda, *The Teachings of Don Juan* (New York: Simon and Schuster,1984). Robert Pirsig simplifies the entire process again by analogy: "The machine that appears to be "out there" and the person that appears to be "in here" are not two separate things." (Robert Pirsig, *Zen and the Art of Motorcycle Maintenance* (New York: Bantam Books, 1974).

[114] A. P. Sinnett, *The Pyramids and Stonehenge* (London: Theosophical Publishing House, 1970). Stuart Piggott, *The Druids* (London: Thames and Hudson, 1988).

time of the year when the temple was used as a calendar system for agricultural planning. Sacred blood on the land, a Druid ritual, is also a reoccurring ritual for other ethnic cultures as well for consecrating the land as a site for the home. Now, a fence had to be built around the site to protect graffiti writing from being written on the walls of the stones by vandals and a patrol added in the evening to stop orgies at the site.

Further South from Stonehenge stands the Avebury circle, a collection of standing stones in another circular form, similar to the form at Stonehenge.[115] Here, however, an indented outer circle or moat around the rocks adds a new dimension to the aesthetic experience. Farmers in the area believe the pit around the rocks was created by a "footprint" of the Celtic gods upon the earth, and worshippers erected the stones to worship them, another phallic, Freudian Father image.[116] The dairy farmers in the region allow their cows to roam freely around the rocks in the moat, and they testify the cows produce better and more milk than others. Geographers have attempted to explain these circular pits as "faults" in the land on an empirical level, but it does not account for the perfect circular shape. This writer sat in one of the hollowed rocks, carved by the winds of Nature, and felt the experience of being in "Mother Nature's cradled arms," safe, secure, and steadied.

Continuing my journey searching for power spots in England, I reached Silbury Hill. The Hill was a mound, spiraling upward, with a trail continuing upward from the bottom around the hill.[117] The fence around the monument read, "No climbing," but, not being a legalist, I had a calling to climb to the top. Once on top, I could see Avebury Circle and Stonehenge from the Hill. I had a complete picture, a nexus of power spots, and I was in the middle of the energy center. Again, I felt the maternal calling of Mother Nature and I realized now that Silbury

---

[115] R. J. C. Atkinson, *The Prehistoric Temples of Stonehenge and Avebury* (London: Pitkin Pictorials, Inc., 1980).

[116] John Sharkey, *Celtic Mysteries: The Ancient Religion* (New York: Crossroad Publications, 1981).

[117] Morris Marples, *White Horses and other Hill Figures* (Gloucester: Alan Sutton Publishing, Ltd., 1981).

Hill was an enormous breast--a maternal symbol, feeding my soul.[118] Here was Mother Earth, Gaia, the Goddess figure, present in my living experience. On the other hand, paradoxically, the view from the top also revealed scores of agricultural plots and cows roaming on typical rural farms. "Feed my sheep" (John 21:17) takes on a new meaning when we are fed spiritually and physically from the land.

Another upward, spiral maze is the Glastonbury Tor, Somerset, England. The pilgrimage/journey motif reoccurs often in Great Britain. Chaucer's *Canterbury Tales* embodies a pilgrimage concluding at Canterbury Cathedral, another power spot on the leyline journey. Jamie George of the Gothic Image Book Store, my guide in Glastonbury, informed me in an interview that Celtics believed Jesus Christ made a pilgrimage to Glastonbury and was educated in the temple at Glastonbury Tor. Glastonbury was a focal, power spot where all points converged: King Arthur legends, Celtic legends, Christian legends, Druid legends, and even Astrological legends. Glastonbury is surrounded by 12 hills (signs of the Zodiac) with the Tor or tower being the center of the region. Each hill has the morphology of its corresponding sign. Wearyal Hill, Pisces, the fish, has trees lining its humped appearance, notably the Holy Thorn Tree, planted by Joseph of Arimathea from the crown of thorns on Christ's head.[119] As the mists set upon this region, eerie veil

---

[118] Harvey Solganick, Theories, *Translations, Truths: Freud's Search for the Soul* (Heidelberg: University of Heidelberg International University, unpublished manuscript, 1988).
Freud also saw images of sexuality and relationships in art objects. His collection in the Freud Museum, London, reveals his search for aesthetic, cultural experiences, not merely a scientific method. [Lynn Gamwell and Richard Wells, Sigmund *Freud and Art: His Personal Collection of Antiquities*, Freud Museum, London, Introduced by Peter Gay (New York: State University of New York, 1989).]
[119] Mary Caine, *The Glastonbury Zodiac: Key to the Mysteries of Britain* (Ashford, England: Flexishape Books, 1978).
Frances Howard-Gordon, *Glastonbury: Maker of Myth.* (Glastonbury: Gothic Image Books, 1982).

envelopes the hills in a Zen experience of illusion/reality, where legend and modern life meet.[120]

At Chalice Well, Glastonbury, one finds the symbol of interlocking circles on the gate, representing the eternal Christ, but also the Gordian knot cut by Prince Arthur.[121] C. S. Lewis studied Medieval Literature and was enthralled with the King Arthur legends. As the water flows down the hill, it picks up mineral deposits, turning the water a reddish color of blood. At the base of the well, a Glastonbury local filled his water jug, telling me this is the water from the Holy Grail in the King Arthur legend, containing the blood of Christ, buried underneath Chalice Well gardens somewhere, and it has miraculous healing powers. I sprinkled some water on my forehead and it had a cooling, soothing effect on me. I drank some water and it settled my thirst. "Thirst, no more!"

Jamie, our guide like Vergil, guided me to the foot of Gemini hill and told me to follow the path alone since it was my sign, my mountain. I came to a fork in the path and did not know which one to take ("Two roads diverged in the wood, and I took the one less travelled by."--Robert Frost). Immediately I crossed the path of two snakes mating together and had to turn around to the other path. Afterward, I realized two snakes, two paths, two selves, two identities--Gemini signs! My final ascension was up the Glastonbury Tor hill. Jamie told me to take my time, placing one foot in front of the other, winding up the spiral maze until I reached the top. Doing Zen meditation, I finally reached the pinnacle where I looked down at the bustling city of Glastonbury, with tourists and vacationers running everywhere. Then as sunset approached, the mist settled over the town, enclosing it in its secretive shroud again.

Cornwall, England is a harsh environment with its roaring sea coast line and the wind constantly blowing in your face. Here on a cliff overlooking the sea stands Tintagel Castle, supposedly King Arthur's

---

[120] Marion Bradley, *The Mists of Avalon* (London: Sphere Books, Ltd.,1982).
[121] Greg Stafford. "The Labyrinth and Tor of Glastonbury," *Shaman's Drum* (Summer, 1987), 40-43.

castle. There one can find the round table of the Knights.[122] This castle site is visited as frequently as Elsinore Castle in Denmark where Hamlet's ghost walks each night among the gargoyles of evil power. Below Tintagel are caves eroding into the cliffs by the constant pounding of the sea. As I walked through a cave, named "Merlin's cave," I could hear "voices" as the water rushed through the floor of the cave, smashing against the rocks. Legend says Merlin was encased within the rocks of this cave and you can hear his voice.[123] As I walked outside to the coastline, I heard young children's voices. I was not certain which were real! "Even the rocks will cry out!" (Luke 19:40)

Not far from Tintagel is a lake where the "Lady of the Lake" resides, holding the magical sword, Excalibur. As I looked for signs of a hand holding up a sword in the lake, a fisherman asked me what I was doing here. When I told him, he laughed and told me, "I know nothing, mate, of any women at this lake, but the fishing is bloody good!" I probably would have more luck finding the Lady of the Lake at White Rock Lake in Dallas, Texas, where a mysterious woman was given a ride, disappeared from the back seat of the car, leaving only water in the seat. Later, news reports demonstrated she was someone who drowned before that appearance. Now, White Rock Lake is listed as a power spot. [124]At Pyramid Lake, Nevada, nestled in a tufa rock formation, I dreamed about Paiute Indians being massacred, only to find out later in the museum that my dreams were true in the past history of that land.[125] It appears that water, from Chalice Well, from Merlin's cave, from lakes,

---

[122] Sir Thomas Malory, *LeMorte d'Arthur: King Arthur and the Legends of the Round Table,*
Transl. by Keith Baines (New York: New American Library, 1982).
[123] T.H. White, *The Book of Merlyn: The Unpublished Conclusion to the Once and Future King*
(New York: Berkeley Books, 1978).
[124] Loren Coleman, *Curious Encounters: Phantom trains, Spooky spots, and other Mysterious Wonders*
(Winchester, MA: Faber and Faber, Inc., 1985), 154.
[125] Sessions S. Wheeler, *The Desert Lake: The Story of Nevada's Pyramid Lake* (Caldwell, Idaho: University of Idaho Caxton Press, 2001).

has a powerful effect on the consciousness, just as my experiences with circular formations, spirals, and maternal attributes of nature. "I am the rivers of life" (Revelation 22:1).

As I journeyed across the water to Scotland, I reached the Hebrides islands, emanating enormous geomagnetic forces. Iona was a place where Celtic crosses and ruins coexist with the Christian Abbey. The wall surrounding the Abbey had stones arranged in a peculiar form of triangles, creating the image of a female fetish, or Goddess, from Celtic legends.[126] As I climbed to the top of the hill on this island, I found a spring of fresh water.[127] Exhausted, I was refreshed and renewed again by the water. In my solitude, the only creature stirring was a sheep who had climbed to the top to drink the water. I thought why does this sheep just climb to drink here, when I must find significance and meaning in my hard journey? As I returned to the Abbey, the priests in their long, black robes were a stark contrast to the white, innocent sheep. Then I thought of the black dung from the white sheep and the white purity from the black-robed priests. "I once was lost, but now I am found" (Psalm 119: 176).

My final stop in Scotland was the Island of Jura.[128] Here George Orwell had written *1984*, a novel of totalitarian ugliness and violence, while Jura was a peaceful, beautiful place to be.[129] Here one is isolated, having to ride the mail truck to get to the ferry boat. When I returned to London, I continued my research at the University of London Tower Library, the model for Orwell's Ministry of Propaganda. Then in reflection, I realized propaganda could no longer work its didactic

---

[126] John G. Dunbar and Jan Fisher, *Iona* (Edinburgh: Royal Commission on the Ancient and Historical
Monuments of Scotland,1983).

[127] Fiona Macleod, *Iona* (Edinburgh: Floris Books, 1982).
Macleod later described the hill where I had this experience: "There is a spot on Iona that always had a strange enchantment for me. Hidden is a little pool. From generation to generation this has been known, and frequented, as the Fountain of Youth," (31-2).

[128] Gordon Wright, *Jura: A Guide for Walkers* (Jura Isle: Sproat Printers, 1983).

[129] George Orwell, *1984* (New York: Signet, 1948).

dogma on my consciousness. It was I who interacted between the objects of Nature, the power spots, along different points of the leyline journey I had chosen. The veil, the crack between worlds, opened up as my imagination slipped into the realm of the Lady of the Lake, as the mists of Avalon surrounded me and I disappeared, only to find myself again in these writings, as they became words on pages, objects of power spots themselves.[130] "And I saw a new heaven and a new earth; for the first heaven and the first earth were passed away" (Revelation 21:1). I realize like Lewis that the imagination is a step toward faith in other worlds, other kingdoms, and ultimately toward the kingdom of Heaven. However, Christianity is not just a matter of imagination, but of reasonable faith.

---

[130] Marcus and J. Clifford, *eds. Writing Culture* (Berkeley: University of California Press, 2012).

Toward Theism and Mere Christianity

In 1929, Lewis became a theist: "You must picture me alone in that room in Magdalen, night after night, feeling, whenever my mind lifted even for a second from my work, the steady, unrelenting approach of Him whom I so earnestly desired not to meet. That which I greatly feared had at last come upon me. In the Trinity Term of 1929 I gave in, and admitted that God was God, and knelt and prayed: perhaps, that night, the most dejected and reluctant convert in all England."[131] Lewis accepted a Christian worldview: a theistic system of rational coherence of biblical revelation as defined by Carl Henry, including a narrative of creation, fall, and redemption. He opposed the "poison of subjectivity" pervading our culture, reducing him to what Dorothy Sayers calls "personal piety." The subjective, personal, and emotional flirtation with other ideas like mysticism, Theosophy, mysticism, and Pantheism was over. Lewis was headed toward a rational belief in God, culminating in an experience of personal revelation, that Christianity was the myth made real and that Christ was the true god who suffered on the cross, not for his own sins, since He was sinless, but for Lewis's sins and for our sins. All the road before him was a journey seeking God while God was seeking him.

---

[131] C. S. Lewis, *Surprised by Joy* (New York: Harcourt Brace, 1966), Chapter 14, 266.

Implications for Evangelism and Discipleship

What lessons can we learn from the adolescent, youth, and education of C. S. Lewis? How can we apply his life discoveries to a model for evangelism and discipleship?

1. *The world is Reality with its objective existence that can be truly known by us, a world created by a Creator who infused reality with His presence.* The world is full of God's glory, His Shekinah glory, since the Light of the world reveals the Truth. We see the rays of the Sun, but do not look directly into the Sun, but still believe it is there. The great "I AM" is the existence of reality and this is my Father's world. We want to desire the true God, in a personal relationship, not merely the rational understanding of God, since only God is omniscient, and we are fallen creatures. Hence, we must love God with all our heart, mind, and soul. For Lewis, we learn what we know, by discovering what we do not know.

2. *By studying other worldviews, philosophies, and cultures, we learn about our own true Christian worldview.* Even though some views are repellant to us and we disagree with them, we recognize we cannot limit the knowledge of God, nor comprehend all of its wisdom. However, education allows us to explore the wonders of God's creation, including our minds, and theology allows us to approximate what doctrines we should believe, and God has given us a gift of the Holy Spirit to guide us and God's Word in the Bible to test the spirits. Questioning is good for the strength of the soul and should be the basis for evangelism. Apologetics defends the faith but does not repress other opinions for exploration.

3. *Love guides us through the search for our soul and our pride gets in the way since we fear the rejection or removal of those closest to us in worldly love.* Evangelism and discipleship should be conducted in love (1 Peter 3:16), not just argumentation.

4. *Thus, an apologetic against the atheist should consist of the following principles*:

1) Never at first attack the atheist's ideas, but demonstrate the atheist has a religion also since "a-theism means a humanist stand against God. ("Only a fool says in his heart there is no God" (Ps.1:4). Everyone has a presuppositional "faith" in something or someone.

2) Never attack the personality of the atheist but be ready to interpret and analyze what the atheist is saying or claiming. (Love the sinner but hate the sin.)

3) Have reverence for the atheist who is one of God's creatures, but does not yet know the Father, adopted in the family of God as a child of God. Be willing to learn from the atheist his or her experiences and problems as a human being. (Even while you were still a sinner, Christ died for you.)

4) Let the Holy Spirit soften the heart and ears of the hardened atheist. You can plant the mustard seed to let the atheist think about God.

Discovering the Classic Apologetic Works of C. S. Lewis

The Abolition of Man (1943)

In the postmodern day of relativism today, one can hear the refrain in any discussion group claiming, "Everything is relative!" This absolute statement is ironic and moronic to C. S. Lewis as a contradiction rationally. The pursuit of ethics, or right or wrong, is substituted by "tolerance" and changing, evolving guidelines, rather than actual rules and doctrines for beliefs. In *The Abolition of Man*, Lewis explores the issue of relativism, a simple position without philosophical depth, and a dangerous idea, since blind obedience to relativism causes people to lose their humanity, becoming "men without chests." The chest protects the heart of mankind as well as our driving motivations of the will. Contemporary mankind does not look to God for absolute rules and values for behavior, but either establishes a new idolatry, "scientism," or turns to programmers or conditioners for their behavior, usually "psychobabblers" or politicians using science for controlling people, called "*scientocracy*" by Lewis.

Lewis begins his book, based on the lectures at Durham University in 1943, by examining the educational textbook teaching English, changing the names of the authors to Gaius and Titus in *The Green Book*. To refute the relativism expressed in the English language, Lewis develops a philosophy of natural law, advocating an absolute right and wrong found in universal principles of Nature, called "The Tao." Christianity usually turns to Theism as he does in his argument defending absolute values, morality, and natural laws revealed by God or "general revelation." One can find the natural law historically in all religions, according to Lewis. Lewis includes the philosophers including Plato, Aristotle, Augustine, and Aquinas, as founders of the natural law concept from both the Western Greco-Roman and Judeo-Christian backgrounds in the history of ideas. As a professor teaching the history of ideas in the great books of the Western World and developing an understanding of engaging our Western civilization and other cultures, like Confucianism and Hinduism, Lewis inspires my teaching of worldviews. He attempts to claim people value opinions as emotions, not truth, and become thus insignificant as values in themselves. Education needs a balance between "intellectualism" and creativity. The Tao gives us a sense of virtues, duty, and justice objectively, not with the poison of subjective emotions, but with rigorous examination through rationality and logic. However, we can sterilize our emotions so much that we no longer feel guilt or shame for our passions becoming what Aldous Huxley calls "noble savages" in *Brave New World*. We become useful practitioners without reflective thoughts or steadfast emotions, a philosophy advocated by American Pragmatists like William James, John Dewey, and applied in constructivism education systems.

However, in his transition from philosophical wisdom to Theism, to Christianity, Lewis admits all the answers are not discovered by human systems of philosophy alone. During his years of study at Oxford University in the 1920's, Lewis wrote a dissertation on the predominance of moral value, but did not associate morals with God, but nevertheless believed in what philosophers call the 'Absolute.' Lewis "distinguished this philosophical "God" very sharply from the 'God of popular religion.'"[132] The Holy Spirit, however, worked on the faith of Lewis so that by 1929, he realized his steps toward Christianity and rational "cerebral" acceptance of the true God: "As the dry bones shook and came together in that dreadful valley of Ezekiel's, so now a philosophical theorem, cerebrally entertained, began to stir and heave and throw off its graveclothes, and stood upright and became a living presence. I was allowed to play at philosophy no longer."[133]

Our society cherishes the trained emotions from teachers or conditioners, giving power to our heads over our impulses and instincts, what Aristotle and Plato call our appetites. For example, a Christian allows the Holy Spirit to guide his appetites or "flesh." Lewis writes, "The head rules the belly through the chest." Then humans should control the emotions connected to the intellect in a holistic, integrated way, making us different as Lewis states than the apes (his criticism

---

[132] C. S. Lewis, Surprised by Joy, Chapter IV.
[133] C. S. Lewis, *Surprised by Joy,* Chapter XIV.

of Darwinism and evolution). Lewis claims, "We make men without chests and expect of them virtue and enterprise." We need instead an absolute, objective moral ethic or code beyond time and culture. W.A. Criswell told me often, "The Word of God stands forever." Lewis rejects the postmodern turn toward relativism, instinct alone, and creating a "new value" for mankind in a progressive, evolutionary, Nietzschean superhuman construction. In addition, Lewis rejects the postmodern politics of the deconstructionists who want a totally free society with no rules except those defined by their power like Mikel Foucault and Francois Lyotard. Christianity allows us to control our sin nature of selfishness and power. We are not animals alone with our instincts and impulses. If we continue this path of self-destruction and ignore Lewis's control or the Tao, "Man's final conquest has proved to be the abolition of Man." Lewis gives us the choice: "Either we are rational spirit obliged to forever obey the absolute values of the *Tao*, or we are mere nature ruled by instinct and natural impulses." Extrapolating the common moral statements from different religions, Lewis demonstrates how these moral values are discovered in every religion from their worldviews.

In Part Two, Lewis explains the Tao more specifically as a validity of moral judgements. He refutes those who argue for denying these virtues since they are making moral judgements themselves in denying absolutes. Finally, in Part Three, Lewis proposes a possible tyranny of the world where the conditioners or programmers no longer believe in an objective truth. Tyranny becomes the will to power, with societal elites attempting to make society in their own image, not by the natural law given to mankind as a gift from God. This rational approach to understand the first principles of morality was a result of Lewis's study of Medieval thought, emphasizing the uniting of faith and reason, and appears again in *The Discarded Image* as well as in the *Chronicles of Narnia*. Lewis is prophetic in foreshadowing the modern economics, politics, psychology, and sociological movements in our contemporary world, as we suffer a moral emptiness and exaltation of selfishness in our own reality. *The Abolition of Man* is one of Lewis's classic works, as Peter Kreeft calls it one of the five books to read to save Western Civilization;

however, Lewis notes, "it is almost my favorite among my books but in general has been almost totally ignored by the public."[134] We cannot ignore his warning.

Miracles (1947)

We wonder if the time for miracles is over today. Worse, we wonder if miracles ever happened. C. S. Lewis experiences the same skepticism and doubt after reading David Hume, *On Miracles*, the same book I read in my first Philosophy class at the University of Texas. Most university professors take pride in creating skepticism and doubt in new Freshmen in college. James Sire wrote about this shaking experience for the new college student in his book, *Chris Chrisman goes to College and Loses his Faith*. I read Hume as well as the atheist, Bertrand Russell's *Why I am not a Christian*, in my first Philosophy class. Both thinkers seem to have arguments for giving up Christianity since the miracles of the virgin birth, the miracles of the Bible, and especially the resurrection were now suspected. However, a little philosophy is dangerous, but the philosophy of logic, rationality, and apologetics can lead one out of the dark recess of skeptical agnosticism and atheism. C. S. Lewis discovered this by his study with Kirkpatrick, by his philosophical dialogues with the Inklings, and his studies at Oxford in Philosophy. Miracles is an apologetic classic, one of the most difficult of his books to read for some, but worth following the arguments for a certain foundation in Christianity. We can thank Dorothy Sayers for asking Lewis to publish his book on miracles in opposition to scientific idolatry.

David Hume in his book, *Essay on Miracles* (1748), argued against the First Cause of all things, including Miracles. He assumed one could never prove the cause for an event since so many variables take place before the effect occurs. He demonstrated this on a billiard table in at Edenborough University in Scotland, a place I visited and played billiards, attempting to practice his causation theory. I did not know whether the movement

---

[134] C. S. Lewis, *Letters to an American Lady* (Grand Rapids: Eerdmans, 1967), 39.

of my elbow, hands, arms, or even my mechanistic brain, caused the ball to fall in the pockets. Hume restricted any supernatural intervention in the universe. He believed the universe was a limited world like a box, what later was called by Adam Behe, *Darwin's Black Box*. The world is a naturalistic world of sense experiences, called empiricism. Lewis refutes this nonintervention by believing in the supernatural in the first place and giving reasons for his belief. He then explores philosophical arguments for miracles, especially the great miracle in the Bible, God's Incarnation where God took the form of a human in Jesus Christ.

Lewis begins by rejecting atomistic materialism ruled by chance. The atoms move around in your brain as synapses and particles, but that does not explain thought. Rationality is beyond nature. Lewis argues Nature did not produce God, but God produced Nature as an organized thought of Creation, not an accidental chance. Moral laws and rational understanding of the natural law cannot derive only from Nature. Nature requires the intervention of a supernatural force to act upon it (in other words, God). God intervened and sent his Son, Christ, as the Incarnation of God as Man as a miracle. God, through Jesus, alters Nature in miracles by healing, creating, or destroying (the withering fig tree). He then creates other miracles anticipating the resurrection, like walking on water, the raising of Lazarus, and the transfiguration. All these miracles are supernatural to the senses of the natural world. Lewis challenges the arguments against miracles because skeptics think that the character of God or Nature itself excludes them. However, this God is a true one, not an alien invasion from magic or fantasy for Lewis, since God is the sovereign creator of Nature. He believes history cannot prove the miraculous; if we believe miracles to be impossible no amount of historical evidence will convince us. Seeing is not always believing; even Jesus tells doubting Thomas that. Greater is he who believes and does not see. Thus, the miraculous is essential to Christianity since it is precisely the story of a great Miracle. Liberal theology which denies the miraculous is not Christianity. Lewis discovered the true experience of miracles in 1957 when his wife, Joy, was "wonderfully" healed.

Belief in the philosophy of the supernatural is essential for Lewis and has been the foundation of great classical thinkers like Athanasius in the 3rd Century A.D. as well as Aquinas in the 13th century A.D. Both believed there is a divine agency outside the commonly observed order of things (Greek, *logos*). However, most liberal theologians have given up the idea of miracles for scientific idolatry. They look to Georg Hegel who equated God with the Law of Nature. Lewis states in his book on Miracles that we avoid the "little horrid red things" or diversions away from believing in the true supernatural world, reducing all miracles to fantasies of the imagination, or ghosts, falling to the ground floor of naturalism, instead of accepting what Francis Schaeffer called "the upper story" of the spiritual realm.

Mere Christianity (1952)

When I first became a Christian in 1988, I was swept away by what was called The Fundamentalist Movement in religion. Church leaders were calling for a return to the inerrant, inspired Word of God in the Bible. This movement appealed to me since my head was muddled by pools of philosophies, man-made systems of thoughts, and the Fundamentalists could tell me what the fundamentals of religion were about in terms of absolute right and wrong, true and false. The difference in my sardonic, sarcastic, and witty approach drove me to put back the "fun" in "*fun*damental." I enjoyed separating the chaff from the wheat. For such a time as this, C. S. Lewis opened the door to the hallway of rooms in his classical work, *Mere Christianity.* I was searching for the fundamentals of Christianity; not what Mac Brunson called the "fluff" around Christianity. Lewis later called this, "Christianity plus" or "Christianity watered-down." The answer to Christianity was not in the denomination, "Baptist born, Baptist bred, Baptist dead." Most Baptists appeared dead to me in their excitement for their Christianity. Lewis presents Christianity as a whole commitment by adhering to its undeniable truths. Denominations in Christianity are good for refining doctrines but should never be taken as Christianity itself. I was fortunate to teach in secular universities, interdenominational universities, and denominational universities. When I came across differences in doctrines and beliefs, I prayed for them if they were wrong and patient with them hoping to open the door to discovery of the truths of Christianity. My whole career as an educator is based upon this "mere Christianity."

Lewis begins with the classic arguments how you can know God exists, how we can know Jesus claimed to be God, how people change when accepting Christ, what it means to be a Christian, and the doctrine of the Trinity. The first audience for Mere Christianity was a radio audience on BBC based upon his talks from 1941 to1944. His talks were combined into a book in 1952. The reader is learning the essential fundamentals as the reader follows the themes of the book. Lewis wrote the book as a member of the Church of England but avoided controversial questions about denominational doctrines as much as possible, attempting to be positive about Christianity. He adopted the name, "Mere Christianity," from Protestant theologian Richard Baxter (1615-1691) who wrote treatises on the fundamentals of religion. He argues that theological controversies must be put in their proper perspective by having a standard of plain, central ("mere") Christianity. He is not arguing for interdenominational acceptance or ecumenicalism as some have conjectured, but a positive, self-consistent system of common ground. First, he constructs an argument for the existence of God based upon the law of human nature and the need for absolute, objective truth against relative beliefs of right and wrong. Next, he discusses free will which is at the center of the existence of evil and suffering in the world. The transition from evil to sin becomes significant and Lewis gives his example of pride as sin as the complete anti-God state of mind. Lewis does not rely upon psychoanalysis as a cure for "sin," and especially criticizes Sigmund Freud who can claim helping people with specific behavioral problems, but Lewis insists the root of our problems is the underlying morality of people. Then Lewis uses the example of marriage moving from "being in love" romantically to a "quieter love" in a mature marriage, one he developed with Joy Davidman. Ultimately, Lewis strongly defends the claims of Christ, arguing he is not merely a great teacher, a moral example, nor a lunatic, or a liar, He is God! From Christ we acquire a "good infection" from Christ's dying on the cross for our salvation and offers all the free gift of eternal life in Heaven. We spread the gospel as evangelists since we are spreading this good infection of the good news. Hence, we become "little Christs" by imitating him, or becoming more conformed to His image through obedience to the Great Commission. However, it is not by our power that we accomplish this. We are not simply "nice people," but are guided by the Holy Spirit of the Trinity when saved. We have to also become disciples, incorporating the teachings of the cardinal and theological virtues of a believer through the Holy Spirit, the Word of God guiding us. We learn temperance, prudence, justice, and fortitude; hope, faith, and charity (love). We have to love and forgive our neighbors as Christ commanded us, demonstrating our hope and faith consistently, not by emotion alone. Finally, Lewis describes the Trinity as a dance of the "living, dynamic activity of love." The Dance (love) between God the Father and God the Son is more than a feeling--"it's tangible, alive, and a dynamic, pulsating activity." For Lewis, Mere Christianity is essence of the experience of joy.

CHAPTER 3

Maturity and Adulthood: Salvation and Separation

Marriage and Separation: C. S. Lewis and the Apologetics of Marriage[135]

C. S. Lewis represents a case study model of the transformation from a legal, conventional marriage in society to a biblical, spiritual bond of marriage as God intended. His relationship with Joy Davidman produced an opening for the Holy Spirit to move Lewis from a Theism position to a true Christian acceptance of Christianity, to a relational Christianity with the bond of God, man, and woman in matrimony with Joy Davidman. In 1929, Lewis became a theist: "You must picture me alone in that room in Magdalen, night after night, feeling, whenever my mind lifted even for a second from my work, the steady, unrelenting approach of Him whom I so earnestly desired not to meet. That which I greatly feared had at last come upon me. In the Trinity Term of 1929 I gave in, and admitted that God was God, and knelt and prayed: perhaps, that night, the most dejected and reluctant convert in all England."[136]

---

[135] Harvey Solganick, "*C. S. Lewis and the Apologetics of Marriage,*" presented at The Southwestern Regional Conference of the Evangelical Theological Society (New Orleans: New Orleans Baptist Theological Seminary, April 15, 2015).

[136] C. S. Lewis, *Surprised by Joy* (New York: Harcourt Brace, 1966), Chapter 14, 266.

In 1931, Lewis became a Christian: "One evening in September, Lewis had a long talk on Christianity with J.R.R. Tolkien (a devout Roman Catholic) and Hugo Dyson. That evening's discussion was important in bringing about the following day's event that Lewis recorded in *Surprised by Joy*: "When we [Warnie and Jack] set out [by motorcycle to the Whipsnade Zoo] I did not believe that Jesus Christ was the Son of God, and when we reached the zoo I did."[137] Beginning in 1956, Lewis entered into a legal ceremony with Joy Davidman; he married Joy Davidman Gresham on April 23, in a secret civil ceremony when the British Home Office denied continuance of her residency permit. Davidman had converted to Christianity from Judaism in 1948 partly under the influence of Lewis's books, met Lewis in 1952, divorced in 1953, due to her husband's desertion, and later developed bone cancer. After his realization of the biblical, true spiritual sense of marriage, on March 21, 1957, he married Joy in a church ceremony at her hospital bed. Throughout 1957, Joy had experienced an extraordinary recovery from her near terminal bout with cancer. In July of 1958, Jack and Joy went to Ireland for a 10-day holiday. On August 19 and 20, he made tapes of ten talks on The Four Loves in London.[138] Lewis had now realized the true value of Christian love. Joy died on July 13, 1960 at the age of 45, not long after their return from Greece. Lewis found his "joy" in Christ. In 1961,"A Grief Observed," an account of his wife's death and suffering was published. His relationship with Joy Davidman, his loss and suffering, were composed into a play and movie introducing Lewis to multitudes.[139]C. S. Lewis wavered in his Christian faith several times, hardening his heart and mind toward God. As a child, the death of his

---

[137] C. S. Lewis, *Surprised by Joy*, 266.

[138] Bruce Edwards, *Into the Wardrobe: C. S. Lewis Website* (http://cslewis.drzeus.net).

[139] William Nicholson, *Shadowlands* (Wales: Television film, directed by Norman Stone and produced by David M. Thompson for BBC Wales, 1985).
William Nicholson. *Shadowlands*, film, directed and produced by Richard Attenborough (Paramount Pictures, 1993).
Brian Sibley, *Shadowlands: The True Story of C. S. Lewis and Joy Davidman* (Fleming H. Revell, 1985).

mother affected him severely. Again, as a young adult, Lewis buried God in the battlefield, waging his own battle for and against God. Lewis himself said, "The early loss of my mother, great unhappiness at school, and the shadow of the last war and presently the experience of it, had given me a very pessimistic view of existence. My atheism was based on it"[140]. Finally, as an older man, Lewis was stricken by the death of his wife, Joy Davidman, and reconstituted his faith in God after a period of confusing despair. However, all these psycho-biographical and psycho-historical experiences also made Lewis into a stronger man of faith. As a child, he "put away childish things;" as a young adult, he dedicated himself on the battlefield to the "glory of God;" and as an older, mature Christian, after "many trials and tribulations," he was drawn closer (what Lewis calls *Sehnsucht*) to God through his "mere Christianity." Thus, with all the road before him, his journey, was not only a personal growth in Christianity, but also an apologetic model for defending the faith against agnosticism and atheism, for himself, but also for others.

Lewis, as a "reluctant convert," probably became a cumulative case apologist, searching for the existence of God in his life. At times, Lewis would even turn to mysticism as a phase for his agnostic inquiry, but this phase could not last for the master apologist. According to David C. Downing, "Ultimately, the contemporary trend in world mysticism must be found wanting, both for its logical inconsistencies and for its empty promise of *gnōsis* without *kenōsis*, the gaining of knowledge without the losing of self"[141]:

> I was thinking about imagination and intellect and the unholy muddle I am in about them at present: undigested scraps of anthroposophy and psychoanalysis jostling with orthodox idealism over a background of good old Kirkian rationalism. Lord what a mess! And all

---

[140] Nicholi Armani, " C. S. Lewis and Sigmund Freud Debate God, Love, Sex, and the Meaning of Life," *The Question of God: School Days* (PBS: Macmillan Free Press, 2003).

[141] David C. Downing, *Into the Region of Awe: Mysticism in C. S. Lewis* (Intervarsity Press, 2005), 148.

the time (with me) there's the danger of falling back into most childish superstitions, or of running into dogmatic materialism to escape them.[142]

Ultimately, Lewis gains both the knowledge of being a Christian and the loss of the old creature, becoming the new creature in Christ.

After Joy Davidson's bout with cancer, its regression, and its eventually overcoming her with death, Lewis writes: "I maintained that God did not exist. I was also very angry with God for not existing. I was equally angry with Him for creating a world." [143] But after realizing that "Pain insists upon being attended to. God whispers to us in our pleasures, speaks in our consciences, but shouts in our pains. It is his megaphone to rouse a deaf world"[144], Lewis realizes: "I know now, Lord, why you utter no answer. You are yourself the answer. Before your face, questions die away. What other answer would suffice? Only words, words; to be led out to battle against other words. Long did I hate you, long did I fear you."[145]

Having realized he would soon forget the face of his beloved wife, Lewis understands that he will recognize her spirit, her soul, in the afterlife. Although he will not be married to her in Christ's kingdom, as she is the bride of Christ, he has learned to grow and be more like Christ in this world by his relationship through marriage. C. S. Lewis finds not only the love of Christ, but also the love of Joy Davidman, and then loses both loves for a period of time in his search for the soul. This loss and recovery is captured in two of his famous works: *Till We have Faces* (1956) and *A Grief Observed* (1961). From the literary work, *Till We have Faces*, C. S. Lewis represents, in the form of the novel, an inquiry into the mythic imagination, borrowing from the source of *The Metamorphoses* in Greek mythology. In *The Metamorphoses*, Cupid forbade Psyche to see his face, a forbidden love. A re-visioning of the

---

[142] C. S. Lewis, *All My Road Before Me: The Diary of C. S. Lewis, 1922-1927*, edited by Walter Hooper and Owen Barfield (Mariner Books, 1991), xi.
[143] C. S. Lewis, *Surprised by Joy* (Harcourt Brace, 1966), 115.
[144] C. S. Lewis, *The Problem of Pain*, 70.
[145] C. S. Lewis, *Till We Have Faces* (Harcourt Brace, 1980), 308.

classical myth of Cupid and Psyche, *Till We have Faces* creates a picture of a "heathenish world, dark, fanatical, and barbarous, yet illumined by an abiding if abrasive love."[146] Psyche or Istria radiates beauty in her face and in her surroundings, whereas Orual, her sister, wears a heavy veil to hide her hideous face. Psyche is carried by the West Wind to a castle in another world, invisible to this world, where her husband forbids her to see his face. Orual, jealous of her love, finds Psyche and convinces her to light a lamp to see her husband's face. The man with the beautiful face tells Orual, that Psyche must now wander with sorrow all over the world. Orual confesses her sin, asking the gods, how can the gods meet me until men have faces, until men present themselves as they authentically are, without pretense. Orual is then transformed into Psyche, the beautiful one. Possessive, enveloping, egoistic love and jealousy are transformed into a devotional, divine, and agape love. The love being taken away becomes the love given to one another. Psyche follows C. S. Lewis' advice: "But think, Psyche. Nothing beautiful hides its face. Nothing honorable hides its name. In your heart you must see the truth, however you try to brazen it out with words."[147]

Thus, Lewis struggles in his work, *Till We have Faces*, between the psyche, the soul, its encounter with the divine, and our inability to express it in words. He creates a mythic land and motif for expressing a metalinguistic experience in his novel since words become a struggle to express the truth in Christ's face:

> I know now, Lord, why you utter no answer. You are yourself the answer. Before your face, questions die away. What other answer would suffice? Only words, words; to be led out to battle against other words. Long did I hate you, long did I fear you...[148]

Lewis uses the image of the face as an identity of the person, an

---

[146] Ovid. *The Metamorphoses*, transl. Anthony S. Kline (http://ovid.lib.virginia.edu/trans/Ovhome.htm)

[147] C. S. Lewis, *Till We Have Faces* (Harcourt Brace, 1980), 66.

[148] C. S. Lewis, *Till We Have Faces* (Harcourt Brace, 1980), 66.

image forgotten in loved ones departed, but remembered in the visage of their real persona personalities. In *A Grief Observed*, Lewis referred to the loss of his wife, Joy Davidman, as one whose face I cannot see, when going through his period of grief and loss of faith. Lewis observes, "In a few minutes I shall have substituted for the real woman a mere doll to be blubbered over. Thank God the memory of her is still too strong (will it always be too strong?) to let me get away with it." As he looks up in the night sky, Lewis can "nowhere find her face, her voice, her touch… she died." He then develops his theory of the imagination, a bundle of impressions "crowd into our memory together and cancel out into a mere blur."[149] Relating to the lost face of Joy, Lewis juxtaposes the ordinary experience of seeing faces in a crowd with the loss of a loved one's face:

> I have no photograph of her that's any good. I cannot even see her face distinctly in my imagination. Yet the odd face of some stranger seen in a crowd this morning may come before me in vivid perfection the moment I close my eyes tonight…We have seen the faces of those we know best so variously, from so many angles, in so many lights, with so many expressions…I wanted to fall in love with my memory of her, an image in my own mind!

C. S. Lewis, in *A Grief Observed*, warns us about images:

> Images of the Holy easily become holy images— sacrosanct. My idea of God is not a divine idea…The Incarnation is the supreme example; it leaves all previous ideas of the Messiah in ruins. And most are 'offended' by the iconoclasm; and blessed are those who are not. [150]

It is only when he reestablishes his faith with a stronger relationship

---

[149] C. S. Lewis, *A Grief Observed* (New York: HarperSanFrancisco, 1989), 66.
[150] C. S. Lewis, *A Grief Observed* (New York: HarperSanFrancisco, 1989), 66.

with Jesus that Lewis remembers her face, not as an image to be idolized, but as a real relationship with a person. Images for Lewis are not important, but merely connections or links to the real person. He compares his love for his lost wife to his love for Jesus: "I need Christ, not something that resembles Him. I want her, not something that is like her."[151]

So, how do we encounter the saving face of Jesus? By removing the dark veil, the ugliness of our sin, hiding our faces from the *shekinah* glory shining in God's face, we experience the "coinherence," a mutual interchange, a substitution or identification of one person for another. There is total reciprocity, first existing in the Trinity at creation, then with the creation of man's relationship with God's image, lost in the Fall, yet restored to mankind by the "adored substitution of Christ."[152] Like Psyche, fastened to a tree (symbolizing Christ's crucifixion), we die to sin, coming to a new life, seeking the otherworldly life of God's kingdom (*Sehnsucht*). C. S. Lewis explains this phenomenological phantasmagoria of his worshipping Christ:

> I must stretch out the arms and hands of love—its eyes cannot here be used—to the reality, through-across-all the changeful phantasmagoria of my thoughts, passions, imaginings. I mustn't sit down content with the phantasmagoria itself and worship that for Him, or love that for her…The mystical union on the one hand. The resurrection of the body, on the other. I can't reach the ghost of an image, a formula, or even a feeling, that combines them. But the reality, we are given to understand, does.[153]

---

[151] C. S. Lewis, *A Grief Observed* (New York: HarperSanFrancisco, 1989), 66.

[152] Charles Williams and C. S. Lewis, "Arthurian Torso" (https://laurelandelmo. wordpress.com/2013/09/18/arthurian-torso-by-charls-williams-and-c-s-lewis/), 143.

[153] C. S. Lewis, *A Grief Observed* (New York: HarperSanFrancisco, 1989), 66; 70-71.

Just as marriage is the model for relationship in Christianity, the Trinity is the model for relationship, the bonding together of the Father, Son, and Holy Spirit. May the foundations of God's Word be blessed in the sacred bonds of marriage.

A Biblical Apologetic of Marriage

Historically, in the Israelite culture of the Bible, arranged marriage, not romantic love, was considered the "natural state" for men and women with single life an exception to the norm. Marriage is defined as the union of a man and a woman in a permanent relationship[154]. Though a lifelong monogamous commitment is presented as the ideal, polygamous marriages were occasionally known in Old Testament times and carried the same legal and moral rights and responsibilities. God's relationship with his people is described in terms of the marriage bond. The purpose of marriage is part of God's intention for humanity from creation and forms the basis for the family which is the primary unit of society. Where marriage flourishes, it blesses both the couple and the wider community. The following are the biblical propositions of marriage in an apologetic argument:

Marriage is part of God's plan for the human race from creation (Mt 19:4; Mk 10:6; See also Ge 1:27; 1Co 11:11-12). Man and woman are not independent of each other. It is to provide companionship (Ge 2:18; See also Ge 2:20-22; 3:12; Prv 31:10-12). It is to be a committed, exclusive relationship (Ge 2:23-24; See also Mt 19:5; Mk 10:7-8; 1Co 7:2; Eph 5:31). It is a lifelong partnership (Mt 19:6; Mk 10:9; See also Ro 7:2; 1Co 7:39). It is the intended context for raising children (Mal 2:15; See also 1Co 7:14). It will not exist in the life to come (Mt 22:30; Mk 12:25; Lk 20:34-35; 1Co 7:29-31). Marriage is a covenant relationship (Mal 2:14; See also Pr 2:17; Eze 16:8). Sex belongs within marriage (1Co 7:9; See also Ge 29:21). Men who violated virgins were expected to marry them: (Ex 22:16-17; Dt 22:28-29; Dt 22:13-21). A woman was expected to be a virgin when she married since the sexual relationship is exclusive (Dt 22:22-24). Marital unfaithfulness is condemned (Pr 5:15-19; 1Co 6:16; 7:3-5). Love and submission in marriage occur (Ge 29:20; See also Ge 34:3-4; Isa 18:20). Husbands are to love their wives (Eph 5:25; See also

---

[154] M. H. Manser, *Dictionary of Bible Themes: The Accessible and Comprehensive Tool for Topical Studies* (London: Martin Manser, 2009).

Ge 24:67; Isa 1:5; Ecc 9:9; Hos 3:1; Eph 5:28-29,33; Col 3:19). Wives are to submit to their husbands (Ge 3:16; Eph 5:22-24; See also Col 3:18; Tit 2:4-5; 1Pe 3:1-6). Celibacy is a calling from God (1Co 7:7-8; See also Jer 16:2; Mt 19:10-12; 1Co 7:36-38). While Paul commends the unmarried state, for those not so called, it is no sin to marry (Ti 5:11-14).

An apologetic for Christian marriage should be foundational upon the Bible and God's Word, not upon the conventions of a "reformed" society. The precepts of the Bible above serve as an argument for a biblical marriage, and we should as Christians preserve and conserve the foundations of God's plan. The agape love of marriage reflects the love God showed us in the bond between man, woman, and God, beyond the Eros, physical union, and the phileo, friendship relationship. C. S. Lewis and Joy Davidman recognized this love under God as we should also. Nevertheless, Lewis begins his deeper spiritual relationships with friendship, one of the "Four Loves" he unifies in the unconditional love of God.

C. S. Lewis and Aristotle's Virtue of Phileo Friendship:

Finding Friendship in Philosophical Discourse

"We live, in fact, in a world starved for solitude, silence, and private:
and therefore, starved for meditation and true friendship."
— C. S. Lewis, *The Weight of Glory* (*Collected Letters* 1949)

Friendship is the theme of book eight in Aristotle's *Nicomachean Ethics*. He describes friendship as necessary and virtuous, for "not one person would choose to live without friends." [155] Friends become a safe house, guarding the young from error and the old from their weakness. Aristotle lays a blueprint for friendship in book eight and addresses three types of friendships: utility, pleasure, and the virtue of the good: *phileo*. Aristotle argues both friendship for pleasure and utility are fleeting, but friendship based on goodness is everlasting. Although, one can agree, there are distinct levels of friendship; friendship for Christ followers is a command and not an option.

Aristotelian Friendship

Aristotelian friendship encompasses three distinct types of friendship. The first encompasses the utility friendship, when the friendship is based on a common goal or project to complete. The friendship remains intact while they share the common goal. However, once the project is completed, the friendship no longer exists because the need no longer exists. This friendship is common in older men, who no longer care what is pleasurable and seek out what is most beneficial for them at the time. The second form of friendship is the friendship based on pleasure. The two maintain a friendship as long as they share a common interest that brings them pleasure. Once one or both friends no longer seek pleasure in the same way the friendship dies. This friendship is more

---

[155] George Apostle Hippocrates and Lloyd P. Gerson, editors, *Aristotle-Selected Works* (Grinnell: Peripatetic Press, 1991), 515.

common in young men, whose interests rise and fall quickly and seek out the next pleasure in a brief period. Aristotle determines these two types of friendship exist for the sole purpose of oneself and has little or no regard for the other person. These friendships are short lived and dissolve quickly.

However, the third friendship he addresses is both virtuous and everlasting. It is the friendship based on the good. This friendship exists to better the other person and to bring out the good in them. Aristotle defines this as a reciprocal friendship[156]. Each person is equally contributing and equally taking from this friendship. They are not partaking in this friendship for their own good. The goal of this friendship is to bring out the good in each other. Therefore, their ultimate goal in friendship is to help the other person actualize their potentiality of the good in themselves. This is a lifelong goal, which leads to an everlasting friendship.

Aristotle views friendship as a noble thing. He says only a friendship based on the good can avoid slander and brokenness. Both friendships based on utility and pleasures are futile and fleeting. For Aristotle, the only friendship worth pursuing is the friendship based on the good.

The Biblical Perspective

The greatest commandment in the Bible is to love God with all the mind, soul, and strength and the second commandment is "to love thy neighbor as thyself" (Matt 10:23, NKJV).[157] In the Christian faith, friendships take on a key role. Friends are to edify one another (Rom 14:19), bear one another's burdens (Gal 6:12), pray for one another (Jas 5:16), and love each other (Rom 12:10). For Christians, friendships play a significant role in training new believers. For example, if a person knows they have an amazing treasure waiting for them and someone tells them

---

[156] George Apostle Hippocrates and Lloyd P. Gerson, editors, *Aristotle-Selected Works* (Grinnell: Peripatetic Press, 1991), 55.
[157] All biblical references, unless other noted, are from *The Holman Christian Standard Bible* version.

exactly what that treasure is, yet they are unable to read and follow the map, they are in for a long expedition. However, if the same person is taught how to follow the map by a person who has already taken the path that leads to the treasure, they will not only learn how to get to the treasure correctly, they will also have someone to help them in the event of a wrong turn or oncoming storm.

Unlike Aristotle's types of friendships, Christians must maintain one type of friendship, a biblical friendship.[158] Proverbs 17:17 states, "A friend loves at all times ..." Biblical friendship is a commandment. Christ followers are commanded to love their neighbors, their families, and even their enemies (Luke 6:27).

Although Christians maintain one type of friendship, three clear levels can be achieved. These include a friendship with someone who is new in their faith, a friendship with a believer who is a peer, and a mentoring friendship with someone who is more mature in their faith. The Bible also gives some clear guidelines on what Christians should look for when choosing their friends. Proverbs 12:26 says, Christ followers should be careful with the friends they choose, for those who are wicked may deceive them, and Proverbs 15:22 encourages Christians to choose wise counsel, for if they do not their plans will go awry. Finally, Proverbs 27:17 says, "As iron sharpens iron, so a man's countenance sharpens his friend."

For Christ followers, it is vital to maintain biblical friendships. Yet, that does not mean that Aristotle does not have some valuable insights for a lasting friendship. It is easy to draw a parallel between Aristotle's friendship based on the Good and Christian friendship.[159] Although they are not equal in value, they both focus on a selfless motive for friendship, which seems to be the base of an everlasting friendship. Yet, regardless of the parallels one may draw from these two types of friendships, one thing is clear. Aristotle's friendship, with disregard to the type, is

---

[158] George Apostle Hippocrates and Lloyd P. Gerson, editors, *Aristotle-Selected Works* (Grinnell: Peripatetic Press, 1991), 526.

[159] George Apostle Hippocrates and Lloyd P. Gerson, editors, *Aristotle-Selected Works* (Grinnell: Peripatetic Press, 1991), 524.

conditional. However, those who follow Christ understand the value of the unconditional love that has been given to them, through what Christ did on the cross of Calvary. Christians, through seeing Christ's example, can say, "A friend loves at all times" (Proverbs 17:17).

C. S. Lewis on Friendship

C. S. Lewis unites friendship or *phileo* [160]as one of the four loves, with all-encompassing *Agape* love from a Christian perspective (*Four Loves*). For this reason, Lewis' life progresses from intellectual, philosophical love, to a theological relationship with God in Theism, to a personal relationship with Christ as exemplified in his friendships with Kirkpatrick, Barfield, Tolkien, Chesterton, and Davidman. The difference in Lewis from Aristotle's virtue of friendship was his intellectual approach combined with his personal relationships. Friendship models, like W.T. Kirkpatrick and Owen Barfield, influenced his intrigue with atheism, while other models, like C.K. Chesterton, and J.R. Tolkien, inspired his Christianity. Ultimately, Joy Davidman becomes his true companion friend, first sharing philosophical friendship, and then spiritual friendship in marriage.

First, the life and teaching style of W.T. Kirkpatrick influenced C. S. Lewis. William T. Kirkpatrick (1848-1921), a retired headmaster of Lurgan College, Northern Ireland, served as Lewis's tutor during the years 1914-1917. He was a friend of Lewis' father, Albert Lewis, who had himself been tutored by Kirkpatrick from 1877-1879. When Jack Lewis went to boarding school, he failed miserably, and returned to individualized tutoring, living with Kirkpatrick. Oddly enough, as predestined knowledge by a Presbyterian, Kirkpatrick told Lewis' father, "You may make a writer or a scholar out of him, but you'll not make anything else."[161] Kirkpatrick used the Socratic method of teaching, making Lewis think through every experience: "If Jack would

---

[160] C. S. Lewis, *The Four Loves: read by the author,* Word Audio Cassette (Dallas: Word Publishing, 1970).
[161] C. S. Lewis, *Surprised by Joy* (Harvest Books, 1966), 183.

look outdoors and comment that it was a nice day, Kirkpatrick would vigorously call out "Stop!" and require Jack to define a nice day and explain his reasons for labeling this particular day a nice one."[162] This logical positivist approach, applying philosophy and linguistics, allowed Lewis to enter into a dialectical dialogue with his teacher, whom he called a "purely logical entity," "a Rationalist of the old, high and dry, nineteenth-century type"[163], a style Lewis utilized, as well as wrote about himself in *Surprised by Joy*; as the skeptical, rationalistic MacPhee in *That Hideous Strength*; and as Professor Kirke claims, "What are these schools teaching nowadays!" in *The Chronicles of Narnia*. Professor Kirke in *The Lion, the Witch, and the Wardrobe*, is perhaps patterned after Kirkpatrick.[164] Like Lewis, Kirkpatrick was an eccentric, who wore his best clothes gardening on Sundays than for weekday gardening, rebelling against his strict, traditional Presbyterian upbringing. Kirkpatrick not only insisted that Lewis learn French, German, Italian, Greek, and Latin on his own, but would read original literary selections in the original language, such as *Medea* and Dante's *Divine Comedy*. Thus, Kirkpatrick framed Lewis' whole career and interests as a medieval scholar, linguist, and rational philosopher. Even though he admired the intellectual abilities of Kirkpatrick, the atheistic worldview served as a foil, a dialectical counterargument, for Lewis as he struggled with his own faith: "From him [Kirkpatrick] I learned something about the honor of the intellect and the shame of voluntary inconsistency."[165]

Secondly, another atheist engaged Lewis as he wrote a letter to Owen Barfield about his battle for God:

> I was thinking about imagination and intellect and the unholy muddle I am in about them at present: undigested scraps of anthroposophy and psychoanalysis jostling with orthodox idealism over a background of

---

[162] Marvin D. Hinton, and Bruce L. Edwards, "William T. Kirkpatrick," In *The C. S. Lewis Reader's Encyclopedia* (Grand Rapids: Zondervan, 1998), 229.

[163] C. S. Lewis, *Surprised by Joy* 139.

[164] Martha Sammons, *Guide through Narnia* (Harold Shaw Publications, 1979), 89.

[165] C. S. Lewis, *Surprised by Joy*, 173.

good old Kirkian rationalism. Lord what a mess! And all
the time (with me) there's the danger of falling back into
most childish superstitions, or of running into dogmatic
materialism to escape them.[166]

This dogmatic materialism or atheism was identified with the
"Kirkian rationalism" of W.T. Kirkpatrick, and his "childish superstitions"
concerned his belief in magic, mysticism, and pseudo-mythology. For
C. S. Lewis, Christianity won the battle over atheistic materialism,
mysticism, and magic since Christianity was the "real" myth, based on
reality after he demythologized all his other beliefs. Lewis had developed
an apologetic against atheism.

If we apply what C. S. Lewis learned from W.T. Kirkpatrick in
his own journey against agnosticism and atheism, we can apply the
following precepts:

"He never attacked religion in my presence."[167]

"Here was a man who thought not about you but about what you
said."[168]

"My debt to him is very great, my reverence to this day
undiminished."[169]

"He was a hard, satirical atheist and the man who taught me to
think."[170]

As an atheist, Kirkpatrick was described by a student as one whose
"pistol never missed fire; but he gave you the impression that, if it did,
you would be knocked down by the butt-end." [171] The Lewis family loved

---

[166] C. S. Lewis, *The Collected Letters of C. S. Lewis, Vol.1: Family Letters*, 1905-1931
(Harper Collins, 2004, January 18, 1927), xi.

[167] C. S. Lewis, *Surprised by Joy*, 140.

[168] C. S. Lewis, *Surprised by Joy*, 137.

[169] C. S. Lewis, *Surprised by Joy*, 148.

[170] C. S. Lewis, *Miracles: How God intervenes in Nature and Human Affairs* (New
York: Macmillan, 1940), 69.

[171] C. S. Lewis, *The Collected Letters of C. S. Lewis, Vol.1: Family Letters, 1905-1931*
(Harper Collins, 2004), I-3.

W.T. Kirkpatrick, in spite of his atheistic humanism, even until his death on March 22, 1921.[172] In conclusion, the biblical principle of apologetics still is the best classical definition of how to do Lewis's apologetics when respectfully encountering a "hard knock" from the atheist:

> "Do not fear what they fear or be disturbed but set apart the Messiah as Lord in your hearts, and always be ready to give a defense to anyone who asks you for a reason for the hope that is in you. However, do this with gentleness and respect, keeping your conscience clear, so that when you are accused, those who denounce your Christian life will be put to shame." (1 Peter 3:14-16 HCSB)

It is a shame that W.T. Kirkpatrick was such an influence on C. S. Lewis by his teaching style and intellectual abilities, but the "hard knock," Kirk, never answered the knock at the door, opening his heart, mind, and soul to the Lord: "'Lord, open up for us!' He will answer you, 'I don't know you or where you're from'" (Luke 13:25 HCSB). Instead, Kirkpatrick was influenced by the depressed philosophies of Bertrand Russell's *Free Man's Worship* and of Schopenhauer's *World as Will*. However, we do know the faith of C. S. Lewis and from whence he came -- out of the darkened despair of the shadowlands of atheism, into the light of the Lord.

In addition to the atheistic, although rational influence of Kirkpatrick, Owen Barfield attempted to derive a philosophy based upon *Anthropos* or human nature alone.[173] Own Barfield provided Socratic dialogue for Lewis's struggle between Atheism and Theism. In addition, J.R.R. Tolkien and Hugo Dyson were immense influences on Lewis's Christianity. Charles Williams also entered into a philosophical, mystical dialogue with Lewis on the nature of the "Co-inheritance of the

---

[172] C. S. Lewis, *The Collected Letters of C. S. Lewis, Vol.1: Family Letters, 1905-1931* (Harper Collins, 2004), I- 1005.

[173] Owen Barfield. "The Case for Anthroposophy," *The Barfield Reader*, edited by G. B. Tennyson (Wesleyan University Press, 1999), 151.

Trinity."[174] Williams believed in the companionship of the saints, akin to friendship relationship, to truly be spiritual. He proposed an order, Companions of the Co-inherence, who would practice substitution and exchange, living in love-in-God, truly bearing one another's burdens, being willing to sacrifice and to forgive, living from and for one another in Christ.[175]

Lewis became a Christian in an ordinary event: One evening in September, Lewis had a long talk on Christianity with J.R.R. Tolkien (a devout Roman Catholic) and Hugo Dyson. Both Tolkien and Dyson walked often with Lewis along a path discussing philosophical and theological ideas, according to Eric Metaxas. That evening's discussion was important in bringing about the following day's event that Lewis recorded in *Surprised by Joy*: "When we [Warnie and Jack] set out [by motorcycle to the Whipsnade Zoo] I did not believe that Jesus Christ was the Son of God, and when we reached the zoo I did."[176] However, this dialogue opened up the mind of C. S. Lewis, but it was his later encounter with Joy Davidman, opening his heart to a personal relationship with her and with Christ in a bonding love[177].

Friendship was a driving force for C. S. Lewis. Lewis expressed some remorse about his lack of friends and colleagues in the established Oxford faculty and sought outside colleague companionship with selected friends since he never felt fully befriended:

[174] Harvey Solganick, "C. S. Lewis: Angling toward the Trinity as an Anglican," presented to the Evangelical Theological Society National Conference (San Antonio, Texas, November 2016).
[175] Barbara Newman, "Charles Williams and the Companions of the Co-inherence," *Spiritus: A Journal of Christian Spirituality* (9 (1): 1–26. doi:10.1353/scs.0.0043. ISSN 1535-3117.January 1, 2009), 26.
[176] Eric Metaxas, *C. S. Lewis: Mere Christianity,* video (Grand Rapids: Zondervan, 2016).
[177] Harvey Solganick, *C. S. Lewis's Influence on Protestant Evangelism and Discipleship,* Sabbatical Grant at C. S. Lewis Institute (Oxbridge, England, July 2017).

His less than full acceptance both of and by his Oxford colleagues may have been one of the reasons for the eagerness with which Lewis developed close friendships and group relations that were continuous with but also alternatives to his relations with academic colleagues. The most famous of these were with the members of the Inklings, a group that began in 1933 and met regularly until 1949. He also moved between his academic residence in in college and his personal, more "Irish" life in Headington. His lack of full acceptance at Oxford also contributed to his move, after some thirty years of professional life there, to a position at Cambridge University as professor of medieval and Renaissance literature in 1955.[178]

Tolkien and Lewis became great friends at Oxford and shared a love for myth and fantasy:

> Tolkien met C. S. Lewis at an Oxford faculty meeting, May 11, 1926. Lewis wrote in his diary about Tolkien that he was "a smooth, pale, fluent little chap … No harm in him: only needs a smack or so." The relationship developed, and Tolkien invited Lewis to join the Coal Biters Club, which focused on reading Icelandic myths (1927). These and other regular meetings allowed Tolkien and Lewis (at this time an atheist) to talk about issues relating to faith. In 1929, Lewis embraced theism; but it was not till 1931 that he came to believe in Christ as the Son of God. One night, Lewis, Tolkien, and Hugo Dyson were having dinner at Magdalen College. Lewis had difficulty with the parallels in pagan mythology and the Gospels.

---

[178] Wesley Kort, *Reading C. S. Lewis: A Commentary (Oxford:* Oxford University Press, 2015), 6.

Lewis maintained that "myths are lies." Tolkien
argued, "No, they are not." Myths in Tolkien's
view, although they may contain error, also reflect
part of God's reality. They are splintered fragments
of the true light. Only by becoming a "sub-creator,"
inventing myths, can mankind return to the perfection
before the Fall. After a long night, together
they concluded that Christ was the true
myth—the myth become fact—revealed in history.
Soon afterwards, Lewis came to believe in Christ.
Lewis wrote in a letter to Arthur Greeves with respect
to his new faith, "My long talk with Dyson
and Tolkien had a great deal to do with it."[179]

The gathering of these friends becomes the "Inklings," where true
love of learning and discussions occur. The spirit of *phileo* becomes a
shared Barnabas, encouraging experience for the group:

One of Tolkien's favorite meetings was his time with
the "Inklings." This informal group met on Tuesday
mornings at the Eagle and Child pub and on
Thursday nights in Lewis's sitting room at Magdalen
College. At night, tea was served, pipes lit, and
inevitably Lewis would query, "Well, has nobody
got anything to read us?" Then someone would
read a poem, story, or Chapter, followed by praise
or criticism, often punctuated with laughter. There
was no formal membership, but regular attendees
were Lewis, Tolkien, Warren Lewis, Dr. Harvard,
Owen Barfield, Hugo Dyson, and Charles Williams.
For instance, Tolkien would read from sections of
a work in progress—*The Hobbit*—and later he read

---

[179] Art Lindsley, *Profiles in Faith: J.R.R. Tolkien. Knowing and Doing* (C. S. Lewis
Institute, 2002), 2.

Chapters of *The Lord of the Rings* to the group. Tolkien says of Lewis's impact on *The Silmarillion* that it was not so much a matter of the influence of his comments but the sheer encouragement of Lewis that kept him going through the lengthy process of writing.[180]

Fourthly, G.K. Chesterton shared a Christian friendship with Lewis in his Orthodox Christianity. Like Lewis, Chesterton transitioned from agnosticism to mysticism to Orthodox Christianity. Chesterton opposed the radical subjectivity in the artistic movement of impressionism, and like Lewis, turned to a rational Christianity. In fact, Chesterton declares "Why should I listen to you, materialists and skeptics?"[181] Nietzsche, Marx, and Atheism led nowhere for him. He found a conversational ear, however, in conversations with C. S. Lewis: "Though certainly famous in his day, Chesterton gained even more recognition after his death in 1936. Much of this acclaim stems from the praise of C. S. Lewis, who hailed Chesterton as a model and credited Chesterton's religious history *The Everlasting Man* with influencing his conversion to Christianity."[182]

Finally, Lewis reaches the pinnacle of friendship in his relationship with Joy Davidman. Lewis was intellectually accepting Jesus as God and Theism as his prevalent theology until the death of his wife, Joy Davidson, allowed him to have a personal relationship with Jesus Christ after his grief was observed:

> On April 23, 1956, he entered into a civil marriage with Joy at the Oxford Registry Office for the purpose of conferring upon her the status of British citizenship to prevent her threatened deportation by British migration authorities. In December, a bedside marriage was performed in accordance with the rites of the Church of England in Wingfield Hospital. Joy's death was

---

[180] Art Lindsley, *Profiles in Faith*, 3.

[181] G. K. Chesterton, *Everlasting Man* (Ignatius, 2000).

[182] Elesha Cofffman, "Profiles in Faith: G.K. Chesterton," *Knowing and Doing* (C. S. Lewis Institute, 2005), 3.

thought to be imminent because of bone cancer. Joy had converted to Christianity from Judaism in 1948 partly under the influence of Lewis's books and divorced in 1953 due to her husband's desertion. On March 21, 1957, He married Joy in church ceremony at her hospital bed. Throughout 1957, Joy had experienced an extraordinary recovery from her near terminal bout with cancer. In July of 1958, Jack and Joy went to Ireland for a 10-day holiday. Joy died on July 13 at the age of 45, not long after their return from Greece. On August 19 and 20, he made tapes of ten talks on The Four Loves in London. Lewis was elected an Honorary Fellow of University College, Oxford. "A Grief Observed," an account of his suffering caused by his wife's death in 1960, published under the pseudonym of N. W. Clerk. The episode was made into a film, "Shadowlands," increasing the popularity of reading Lewis' works.[183]

Lewis lost his wife, but ultimately not his joy. His relationship with his wife mirrored the relationship with his Lord, Jesus Christ, as he grew from *phileo* love to *agape* love. Lewis experienced the true virtue of love, not *arête,* but *phileo* as a part of *agape* love.

---

[183] John Visser, editor, *Into the Wardrobe: A C. S. Lewis Website, 1994. (http:// www.cslewis.drzeus.net/).*

C. S. Lewis: Losing Face in the Death of Joy

C. S. Lewis finds not only the love of Christ, but also the love of Joy Davidman, and then loses both loves for a period of time in his search for the soul. This loss and recovery is captured in two of his famous works: *Till We have Faces* (1956) and *A Grief Observed* (1961). From the literary work, *Till We have Faces*, C. S. Lewis[184] represents, in the form of the novel, an inquiry into the mythic imagination, borrowing from the source of The Metamorphoses[185] in Greek mythology. In *The Metamorphoses*, Cupid forbade Psyche to see his face, a forbidden love. A re-visioning of the classical myth of Cupid and Psyche, Till We have Faces creates a picture of a "heathenish world, dark, fanatical, and barbarous, yet illumined by an abiding if abrasive love."[186] Psyche or Istria radiates beauty in her face and in her surroundings, whereas Orual, her sister, wears a heavy veil to hide her hideous face. Psyche is carried by the West Wind to a castle in another world, invisible to this world, where her husband forbids her to see his face. Orual, jealous of her love, finds Psyche and convinces her to light a lamp to see her husband's face. The man with the beautiful face tells Orual, that Psyche must now wander with sorrow all over the world. Orual confesses her sin, asking the gods, how can the gods meet me until men have faces, until men present themselves as they authentically are, without pretense. Orual is then transformed into Psyche, the beautiful one. Possessive, enveloping, egoistic love and jealousy are transformed into a devotional, divine, and agape love. The love being taken away becomes the love given to one another. Psyche follows C. S. Lewis' advice:

> But think, Psyche. Nothing beautiful hides its face.
> Nothing honorable hides its name. In your heart you

---

[184] C. S. Lewis, *Till We Have Faces: A Myth Retold* (Grand Rapids: Eerdmans, 1956).

[185] Lucius Apuleius Platonicus (125 A.D.), *Metamorphoses*, edited by Robert Graves (Penguin, 1950).

[186] Nathan Comfort Starr, *C. S. Lewis's Till We Have Faces: Religious Dimensions in Literature* (New York: Seabury Press, 1968), 10.

must see the truth, however you try to brazen it out
with words.[187]

Thus, Lewis struggles in his work, Till We have Faces, between
the psyche, the soul, its encounter with the divine, and our inability to
express it in words. He creates a mythic land and motif for expressing a
metalinguistic experience in his novel since words become a struggle to
express the truth in Christ's face:

> I know now, Lord, why you utter no answer. You are
> yourself the answer. Before your face, questions die
> away. What other answer would suffice? Only words,
> words; to be led out to battle against other words. Long
> did I hate you, long did I fear you...[188]

Lewis uses the image of the face as an identity of the person, an
image forgotten in loved ones departed, but remembered in the visage of
their real *persona* personalities. In A Grief Observed[189], Lewis referred to
the loss of his wife, Joy Davidman, as one whose face I cannot see, when
going through his period of grief and loss of faith. Lewis observes, "In
a few minutes I shall have substituted for the real woman a mere doll to
be blubbered over. Thank God the memory of her is still too strong (will
it always be too strong?) to let me get away with it."[190] As he looks up in
the night sky, Lewis can "nowhere find her face, her voice, her touch...
she died."[191] He then develops his theory of the imagination, a bundle of
impressions "crowd into our memory together and cancel out into a mere
blur."[192] Relating to the lost face of Joy, Lewis juxtaposes the ordinary
experience of seeing faces in a crowd with the loss of a loved one's face:

---

[187] *Till We Have Faces*, 160.
[188] C. S. Lewis, *Till We Have Faces,* 308.
[189] C. S. Lewis, *A Grief Observed (*San Francisco: Harper, 2001).
[190] C. S. Lewis, *A Grief Observed,* 4.
[191] C. S. Lewis, *A Grief Observed,* 15.
[192] C. S. Lewis, *A Grief Observed,* 16.

> I have no photograph of her that's any good. I cannot
> even see her face distinctly in my imagination. Yet the
> odd face of some stranger seen in a crowd this morning
> may come before me in vivid perfection the moment I
> close my eyes tonight...We have seen the faces of those
> we know best so variously, from so many angles, in so
> many lights, with so many expressions...I wanted to
> fall in love with my memory of her, an image in my
> own mind! [193]

It is only when he reestablishes his faith with a stronger relationship with Jesus that Lewis remembers her face, not as an image to be idolized, but as a real relationship with a person. Images for Lewis are not important, but merely connections or links to the real person. He compares his love for his lost wife to his love for Jesus: "I need Christ, not something that resembles Him. I want her, not something that is like her."[194]

Just like C. S. Lewis' search for the spiritual face of Christ, the search for the "real" face of Christ in the realm of aesthetics, art, and architecture, has been controversial.[195] Some, like Peter and Linda Murray, claim, "There is no evidence at all for the actual appearance of Christ, and even 'descriptions' of his physical characteristics are evidently imaginary as well as being much later than the Ascension."[196] Most portraits of Christ are Oriental or Greek (Hellenistic). The Oriental forms incorporate the Jewish features of Jesus: bearded, older-looking, philosophical, with an austere face, staring eyes, and long dark hair.

---

[193] C. S. Lewis, *A Grief Observed*, 19-20.

[194] C. S. Lewis, *A Grief Observed*, 65.

[195] Peter and Linda Murray, eds., "Christ," *The Oxford Companion to Christian Art and Architecture: The Key to Western Art's most Potent Symbolism* (Oxford: Oxford University Press, 1996).
See the *Iconographic Route* for portrayals of the face of Christ.

[196] Peter and Linda Murray, eds., "Christ," *The Oxford Companion to Christian Art and Architecture: the Key to Western Art's most Potent Symbolism* (Oxford: Oxford University Press, 1996), 103.

Influenced by these Byzantine images, Caesare Lombroso, a nineteenth-century medical writer, even used Oriental features of the facial cranium to describe the "criminal man" as a Jewish vagabond.[197] The earlier Greek representations attempted to capture the beautiful features, the beardless, young man with curly hair, similar to David the shepherd. From the Gothic period, the suffering image of Christ turned, by the time of the Renaissance and Reformation, into an emphasis upon the gentle, milder image of Christ.

Another group, although smaller, claims to have the authentic image of Christ, or copies of it, made miraculously or by hand. The Shroud of Turin is probably the best-known representative of this group. However, statues of Jesus performing miracles were reported by Eusebius in 323 AD. Veronica's Veil (*vera icon*) was impressed with the image of Christ's face when she wiped his face with her veil as He was carrying the cross. The Mandylion was a cloth said to have been imprinted with the features of Christ and sent to King Abgar of Edessa (now N. Syria). The Flemish painters were inspired by the reported painting of Madonna and Child by Luke. There are also sightings of Jesus' face in glass buildings, autos, and other areas, but these are more suspect and transient in influence. Even a computer-generated image has been attempted to reconstruct the "real Jesus." However, as C. S. Lewis, in *A Grief Observed*, warns us about images:

> Images of the Holy easily become holy images—
> sacrosanct. My idea of God is not a divine idea…The
> Incarnation is the supreme example; it leaves all previous
> ideas of the Messiah in ruins. And most are 'offended'
> by the iconoclasm; and blessed are those who are not.[198]

So, how do we encounter the saving face of Jesus? By removing the dark veil, the ugliness of our sin, hiding our faces from the *shekinah*

---

[197] Gina Lombroso-Ferrero, *Criminal Man, According to the Classification of Caesare Lombroso* (Patterson Smith, 1972).
[198] C. S. Lewis, *A Grief Observed*, 66.

glory shining in God's face, we experience the "coinherence," a mutual interchange, a substitution or identification of one person for another. There is total reciprocity, first existing in the Trinity at creation, then with the creation of man's relationship with God's image, lost in the Fall, yet restored to mankind by the "adored substitution of Christ."[199] Like Psyche, fastened to a tree (symbolizing Christ's crucifixion), we die to sin, coming to a new life, seeking the otherworldly life of God's kingdom (*Sehnsucht*). C. S. Lewis explains this phenomenological phantasmagoria of his worshipping Christ:

> I must stretch out the arms and hands of love—its eyes cannot here be used—to the reality, through-across-all the changeful phantasmagoria of my thoughts, passions, imaginings. I mustn't sit down content with the phantasmagoria itself and worship that for Him, or love that for her...The mystical union on the one hand. The resurrection of the body, on the other. I can't reach the ghost of an image, a formula, or even a feeling, that combines them. But the reality, we are given to understand, does.[200]

Some Protestant theologians fear idolizing the physical face of Jesus: *Like one from whom men hide their faces he was despised, and we esteemed him not"* (Isaiah 53:3). With a hermeneutic of suspicion[201] toward the anthropomorphic figure, suggesting a hint of idolatry, secularization,

---

[199] Charles Williams, *Arthurian Torso* (London: Oxford University Press, 1948), 143.

[200] C. S. Lewis, *A Grief Observed*, 66; 70-71.

[201] Paul Ricoeur calls ideas under suspicion in our consciousness, a "hermeneutic of suspicion." [Paul Ricoeur, *Hermeneutics and the Human Sciences: Essays on Language, Action, and Interpretation* (Cambridge UP, 1981)].

dehumanization, and even a neo-gnostic[202] attitude toward the portrayal of Jesus the man, some are afraid to "turn their eyes upon Jesus, look full in His wonderful face."[203] The purpose of this study was to grasp the multi-faceted faces of Jesus as *persona* of our *psyche*, as portrayed in the Word of God, reflected with the insightful influences of sermons by R.G. Lee[204]; literary writings of C. S. Lewis[205]; and in the aesthetic history of art[206]. The Old Testament portrays the "face" as the "face of the earth" (Exodus 10:5). Although the Hebrew could not look directly into the face of God, the expectation of seeking the face of the Lord means to come into His presence in confession, to believe His word and to seek His fellowship (Ps.27:8). We are made rich by the blessing of God and gaze upon His lovely face (Numbers 6:25). Ezekiel 1:6-11 describes the four aspects of Christ's face:

> Each of them had four faces and four wings. Their legs were straight, and their feet were like a calf's hoof, and they gleamed like burnished bronze. Under their wings on their four sides {were} human hands. As for the faces and wings of the four of them their wings touched one another; {their faces} did not turn when they moved, each went straight forward. As for the form of their

[202] "Gnosticism" was a religious movement popular in the second and third centuries, believing in the higher spiritual knowledge, depreciating the material world (C. Stephan Evans, *Pocket Dictionary of Apologetics and Philosophy of Religion* (Downers Grove: Intervarsity Press, 2002), 49.

[203] Helen H. Lemmel, "Turn Your Eyes Upon Jesus" (1922), http://my.homewithgod.com/heavenlymidis/songboook/turneyes.html.

[204] R.G. Lee, "The Face of Jesus Christ," *Payday Someday and other Sermons*, edited by Timothy and Denise George (Nashville, TN: Broadman and Holman Publishers, 1995), 68-87.

[205] C. S. Lewis, *Till We Have Faces: A Myth Retold* (Grand Rapids: Eerdmans, 1956).

C. S. Lewis, *A Grief Observed* (San Francisco: Harper, 2001).

[206] Peter and Linda Murray, eds., "Christ," *The Oxford Companion to Christian Art and Architecture: The Key to Western Art's most Potent Symbolism* (Oxford: Oxford University Press, 1996).

faces, {each} had the face of a man; all four had the face
of a lion on the right and the face of a bull on the left,
and all four had the face of an eagle. Such were their
faces.

In addition, the four gospels of the New Testament characterize the
four views of Christ:

Matthew explains the lion characteristics of Christ;
Mark describes the ox character; Luke presents the
human character; and John represents the Deity of our
Lord.[207]

Genesis 1:27 states we were created in the image of God, *imago
dei:* "So God created man in His own image; in the image of God He
created him; male and female He created them."; and John 1:14 states
God came in the form of a man, fully human and fully divine: "And
the Word became flesh and dwelt among us, and we beheld His glory,
the glory as of the only begotten of the Father, full of grace and truth."
The intent is not to portray an accurate, realistic portrait of the face of
Jesus, but to present some metaphorical images pointing us toward the
message of God's Word. These symbols and signs, unlike Saussure's
semiotic theory[208], do not become a deconstruction of reality, but reflect
reality itself since God created this reality. Hopefully, in remembrance of
Him, we will gaze upon the face of Jesus, and the finite world will "grow
strangely dim/In the light of His Glory and Grace."[209]

The personal relationship with Christ is not a psychological
projection. I grew up being teased about my name being Harvey when

[207] Walter L. Wilson, *A Dictionary of Bible Types* (Hendrickson Publishers,
1999), 142.
[208] Ferdinand Saussure, *Course in General Linguistics* (New York: McGraw-Hill,
1965).
[209] Helen H. Lemmel, "Turn Your Eyes Upon Jesus," (1922).

compared to the tall rabbit in Mary Stewart's play, "Harvey,"[210] about an imaginary friend to Elwood P. Dowd. However, God is a real person. He is not a human invention, a concept, a theory, or a projection of ourselves. He is overwhelmingly alive, real beyond our wildest imagination or dreams. David tells us He can be encountered or "met": "As the deer pants for streams of water, so my soul pants for You, O God. My soul thirsts for God, for the living God. When can I go and meet with God?" (Ps. 42:1-2) A.W. Tozer wrote:

> God is a Person and as such can be cultivated as any person can. God is a Person and in the depths of His mighty nature He thinks, wills, enjoys, feels, loves, desires, and suffers as any other person may. God is a Person and can be known in increasing degrees of intimacy as we prepare our hearts for the wonder of it.[211]

When we look for the face of Jesus in the art galleries, or in portraits, on nursery walls, in stained glass, in statues, or even in our mind's eye when reading the Bible, "we will get evidence that all its portraits lose their splendor in the greater glory of the face of Jesus Christ."[212] R.G. Lee sums it best when he states:

> We have seen Him in the sacred page. We have seen Him on the artist's canvas. We have seen Him in the light of faith. But we want to see Him as He is.[213]

From R.G. Lee's diaries,[214] we know that he jealously guarded his hours in the study and never entered the pulpit to talk to his people until

---

[210] Mary Chase, *Harvey: A Play in Three Acts* (1944), Snowball Publishing Company, (Accessed August 21, 2017) (http://www.snowballpublishing.com).

[211] A. W. Tozer, "Following Hard after God," In *Pursuit of God* (Camp Hill, PA: Christian Publications, 1982), 13.

[212] R. G. Lee, "The Faces of Christ," 69.

[213] R. G. Lee, "The Faces of Christ," 87.

[214] Timothy George, "Introduction," *Payday Someday*, 7.

he had first talked personally to God, face to face. His treatise, "The Faces of Jesus," reflects a mirror image of Jesus' message to our humanity.

R.G. Lee, in "The Face of Jesus Christ,"[215] describes the multifaceted faces of Jesus that we must seek for the reality of uniting with Christ:

1. The Sad Face: "He was despised and rejected by men, a man of sorrows, and familiar with suffering. Like one from whom men hide their faces he was despised, and we esteemed him not" (Isaiah 53:3). Lee describes the sadness that came from a sinless heart that grieved over men and sorrowed over their foolish and perverse ways.

2. The Shining Face: "And He was transfigured before them: and his face did shine as the sun, and his radiance was white as the light" (Matt. 17:1-2). Jesus was the brightness of God's glory and the express image of His person: (Heb. 1:2-3). "We see the light of Christ on Paul's Journey on the road to Damascus (Acts 91-6).

3. The Stained Face: "Jesus wept" (John 11:35) Jesus wept at Bethany, at the city of Jerusalem (Luke 19:41), in the garden at Gethsemane (Luke 22:41-44). His tears and blood-stained face were for all humanity, as well as his face spit upon (Mark 15:19). Yet, Jesus "hid not my face from shame and spitting" (Isa. 50:6).

4. The Smitten Face: "His visage was so marred more than any man" (Isa. 52:14). "Surely, he hath borne our griefs, and carried our sorrows: yet we did esteem him stricken, smitten of God, and afflicted" (Isa. 53:4). Lee tells us to remember the smitten face where never dwelt a trace of indwelling hate.

5. The Set Face: "And it came to pass, when the time was come that he should be received up, he steadfastly set his face to go to Jerusalem, and sent messengers before his face" (Luke 9:51). Jesus never turned away from his destiny at Calvary.

6. The Scorching Face: "Who do men say that I the Son of man am?" (Matt. 16:13) Often the Jesus of popular thought for Lee is a meek and mild-eyed saint who was always saying gracious things and always doing gentle deeds. The Christ with eyes of flame and feet of brass, as

---

[215] R. G. Lee, "The Faces of Jesus Christ," 68-87.

John of Patmos saw him, is a stranger to some (Rev.20:11). The stern, angry Jesus overthrew the moneychangers in the temple (John 2:15-17).

7. The Shrouded Face: Jesus died, and Joseph of Arimathea went to Governor Pilate and begged for the body of Jesus (Matt.27:58). Lee describes that shrouded face as a banquet for worms.

8. The Seen Face: "Now we see through a glass darkly; but then face to face" (1Cor.13:12). We shall see the faces of loved ones in heaven "awake in His likeness." "As for me, I will behold thy face in righteousness: I shall be satisfied when I awake, with thy likeness" (Ps. 17:15). Lee compares the appearance of Jesus to a family reunion, where there shall be One, however, whose personality shall be dominant.

Therefore, the tension for the Christian remains: "Above all, I want to see Jesus"[216]); however, Jesus tells Thomas and us in response to our skeptical empiricism, "Behold My hands and My feet, that it is I Myself. Handle Me and see, for a spirit does not have flesh and bones as you see I have"(Luke 24:39). We also have to accept Jesus for his perfect humanity and his perfect divinity by faith, until we have faces encountering the many facets of Jesus glorified body:

> Open my eyes, that I may see
> Glimpses of truth Thou hast for me;
> Place in my hands the wonderful key
> That shall unclasp and set me free.

---

[216] Original words and music by Alexandria Williams, "I Want to See Jesus In Every Song I Sing Today," (http://www.geocities.com/alexandria_williams/ Content/iwanttoseeJesus.htm).
I want to see Jesus!
I want to see Jesus!
I want to see Jesus!
In every song I sing today!
And I will walk with Him,
And talk to Him!
Rejoicing in the way!

Silently now I wait for Thee,
Ready, my God, Thy will to see;
Open my eyes,
illumine me, Spirit Divine! [217]

---

[217] Clara H. Scott, "Open my Eyes that I may See," (1865) (www.tagnet.org/
digitalhymnal/en/dh326.html).

Implications for Evangelism and Discipleship

What lessons can we learn from the maturing spiritual life, fellowship, and marriage of C. S. Lewis? How can we apply his life discoveries to a model for evangelism and discipleship?

1. *Marriage is a covenant, a bond, between man, woman, and God, unifying the relationship on a spiritual level, not just a physical one.* C. S. Lewis searches for the remembrance of the physical appearance of Joy's face after her death but realizes he can capture her "spiritual face", her spiritual being or soul she shared with him in this world that will continue eternally. Evangelism works best face to face with personal relationships, but other forms can be utilized by reading the Bible, using media, etc. Discipleship is growing more conformed to the image of Christ as a marriage grows by sharing a prayer life and Bible study with your spouse.

2. *Love is built upon intimacy (Eros), friendship (phileo), caring for one another (Sorge), and encompassed in unconditional love (agape) as a gift from God.* Love is multifaceted just as a marriage is multi-dimensional. C. S. Lewis describes these loves in *The Four Loves*, as a key for understanding eternal love of Christ. He always took a strong stand for Christian marriage for either faithfulness to your partner completely, or else total abstinence in *Mere Christianity*. Those who follow Christ understand the value of the unconditional love that has been given to them, through what Christ did on the cross of Calvary. Christians, through seeing Christ's example, can say, "A friend loves at all times" (Proverbs 17:17). The marriage of Joy and Jack did what any good marriage should do: it made each of them into stronger, more complete human beings. It may have begun as a friendship, but as it grew it eventually explored all the four loves.

3. *For Christians, friendships play an important evangelical and discipleship role in training new believers.* For example, if a person knows they have an amazing treasure waiting for them and someone tells them exactly what that treasure is, yet they are unable to read and follow the map, they are in for a long expedition. However, if the same person

is taught how to follow the map by a person who has already taken the path that leads to the treasure, they will not only learn how to get to the treasure correctly, they will also have someone to help them in the event of a wrong turn or oncoming storm. Personal relationship formations are the foundations for evangelism. C. S. Lewis experienced a friendship with Tolkien, Dyson, Chesterton, Joy Davidman, and others sharing the gospel with him. Friendship was a driving force for C. S. Lewis in his salvation. His friendship and intellectual engagement with Joy Davidman led to love later in their marriage. Joy's last words to her husband were, "You have made me so happy and I am at peace with God."

4. *The purpose of marriage is part of God's intention for humanity from creation and forms the basis for the family which is the primary unit of society, not self-exaltation, and convenient marriages and divorce.* Where marriage flourishes, it blesses both the couple and the wider community. God's plan was initiated with Adam and Eve at the beginning of creation in Genesis. They were separated from God by sin, but our God is a loving, forgiving God and desires his people to be the children of God, adopted into the family of God, repentant of separation from God, and become the "Bride of Christ" unified in the church. C. S. Lewis never gives up his belief in the eternal standard of marriage, but shows mercy and forgiveness by his charity, marrying Joy Davidman, who is divorced, even going against the Anglican Church creed, but finding a minister who still believed in the priesthood of the believers and a repentant heart. Lewis gave her some spiritual understanding regarding her own muddled, violent matrimony, married her for convenience of citizenship, but ultimately realized the spiritual necessity of marriage.

Discovering the Works of Heaven (Love and Reconciliation) and Hell (Divorce and Alienation)

The Four Loves (1960)

Lewis's life is a progressive journey from caring for animals in his garden to friendships with human beings, then ultimately to romantic love and infinitely to unconditional love for God. We know Christ is love and holds all things together with love as a dynamic force of the Trinity and its reconciliation with the Father. Lewis explains his influences of love in his work, *The Four Loves*, by reiterating the Greek concepts of love lasting throughout the courtly love he studied in Medieval literature. He begins with affection, *Storge*, a caring love for animals and nature. After all, all creatures here below are part of the doxology hymn he sang in the church. *Storge* is a nurturing love expressed in motherhood, not lost on his own love for his mother who died of cancer. *Philia*, or friendship, becomes essential for exchanging Platonic ideas with his friends, the Inklings, with Dorothy Sayers, and with Joy Davidman on an intellectual level of philosophical discourse. His love for Joy Davidman grows and matures into *Eros*, or being in love with a special person, developing a love for the Other. However, he concludes the height of love is *Agape*, true unconditional love given to us as a gift from God, allowing us to experience the greatest virtue of all, charity to others with self-sacrifice. For God so loved us He sent his only begotten Son that we shall not perish but have everlasting life. *Agape* unifies all the human loves together as natural loves embedded in divine love. Lewis warns us that idolizing one of the natural loves makes them "false gods" when worshipped on their own without the relationship to divine love. For example, if we attempt to live by *Storge* or affection alone is a dependence upon old habits of feelings like an old shirt you wear, making you prideful, selfish, and self-absorbed. Lewis considers *Philia* or friendship to create innovative ideas by philosophizing, being creative, but again we can create self-interest groups excluding new relationships unless accompanied by entering into an evangelical relationship with others without an aristocratic attitude. *Eros* seeks the loved one, but not merely physically; we can worship the other, however, as a goddess or god, trying to capture the Other by possession, but when *Eros* tries to live for itself apart from divine love, it will become fleeting in one's love. Agape is the answer for love eternally then, leading to the shared intimacy (*Eros*), the friendship (*philia*), and care (*Sorge*) for the Other in a relationship united in marriage under God (*Agape*). In eternity we are the bride of Christ sustained by the *agape* love as a gift in the first place. Our need for love is fulfilled in that God first loved us as a gift-love.

Although C. S. Lewis has been called a "Romantic Rationalist," he allows feelings and emotions to grow into a true love in marriage, especially. Marriage is a lifelong union between man and woman; it is permanent to him in this world. Just as Jesus hates divorce, Lewis also hated divorce and its consequences; however, he also has a forgiving heart, a heart of repentance, since he accepted Joy Davidman's divorce from her marriage. For Lewis, love involves a transition from emotions to action, part of his Anglican upbringing stressing works. The action becomes a symbol of the covenant they made with one another, under God. He equates marriage as a train engine running after the ignited explosion that began it. A renewing of the couple's marriage vows sustains the relationship of their marriage just as a renewal of the spirit. Marriage will have its setbacks, highs and lows, but it lives on filling in the gaps of alienation. The ultimate alienation of the unity is death; however, Lewis recognizes the hope of reuniting with loved ones in heaven. It is divorce that separates and chops up the unity of the body, two becoming one flesh, and the spiritual bond of unity under God dies.

The Great Divorce (1943)

C. S. Lewis creates a fantasy journey about a group of people riding a bus from Hell visiting Heaven on a holiday. He originally read the 17th Century Anglican writer Jeremy Taylor developed the idea of a theological "*refrigeratum*," a holding place of momentary rest from Hell similar to Lewis's reading of Dante's *Purgatorio* in the *Divine Comedy*.

The title originally was *Who Goes Home?* which was based upon the yell traditionally shouted by the guard in British Parliament when preparing to close the doors and end the session. The revised title was an opposing view of William Blake's The Marriage of Heaven and Hell. Blake was a mystic romantic poet who believed loved ones would be reunited in Heaven, but Lewis recognized the biblical view that we are the Bride of Christ as Christians in Heaven and there is not a chance of being married in Heaven. Furthermore, divorce was the gap, the chasm existing between those people who are saved and those who reject Christ and follow their own paths instead. The ultimate divorce from this life is death, and the wages of sin paid by unbelievers like those on the bus trip in his fantasy. Evil can be remedied by Christ, but it cannot change into good by one's own power. This ultimate lesson becomes the lesson for evangelizing others and the theme in *The Great Divorce*. George MacDonald becomes the guide for the bus journey just as Dante employed Virgil and Beatrice as the guides for the journey through Purgatory to Paradiso, Paradise in Heaven.

Lewis's strong belief in free will allows the characters to choose to remain in Heaven or they can choose to return to Hell. All return to Hell except one. Many critics believe Lewis believed in universalism, the idea that everyone submits to God, either before or after death, and goes on to live with God in Heaven. His compromise entails purgatory, a Roman Catholic idea that Christians have a stopping point to atone for their sins. Hell, in *The Great Divorce* is a second opportunity for salvation where God brings people to Him, another instance of *Sehnsucht* or God seeking us (Proverbs 8:17).

Lewis portrays Hell figuratively as a real place just as tangible as the world we live in today. We notice the residents of Heaven only focus on Christ, not religion itself, as factually real. However, no quality of Heaven will ever be found in Hell. Hell is a dismal place to live, a grey town, rainy, and in the "twilight zone." People squabble at each other in Hell and resort to living alone in Hell. Christian community is lost. Relationships are sacrificed for independence and individualism. Darwin's social ethic of survival of the fittest is followed. Hell, ultimately, becomes a value of Nothingness, a deconstruction of the world: "All Hell is smaller than one pebble of the earthly world, but it is smaller than one atom of this world, the Real World." Hell becomes our mental prison shutting ourselves up in our own minds. The inhabitants of Hell are distorted and faded images of their past life, transparent ghosts whom you can stare through, a vapor who tries to adhere to earthly life instead of soaring into Heaven. On the other hand, occupants of Heaven are spiritual and solid, majestic and ageless, not self-absorbed with selfishness, and loving creatures like Christ. People in Heaven will share a glowing, glorified body like Christ. Evangelism leads one to this angelic place by accepting Christ.

The characters portrayed in The Great Divorce are warning personality traits to us. Each represents a pitfall of our own choice of walking with the Lord or choosing not to follow His Way:

> I have my rights! Pride and The Big Man: "I've never asked for anything that wasn't mine by rights."

> The Youth with a 'Tude: "The tousle-headed youth felt quite certain that he was going where, at last he would find Recognition and Appreciation." (Hebrews 12:2)

> The bowler-hatted Ghost Materialist: "If I can come back with some real commodities I'd start a business, I'd make a nice little profit." (Mark 8:36)

> The skeptical Theologian Episcopal ghost: "For me there is no such thing as a final answer." (Matthew 18:3)

> The Pessimistic, Hard-Bitten Ghost: "Same old lie. People have been telling me that sort of thing all my life."

The Self-Conscious Woman: "Could you, only for a moment, fix your mind on something not yourself?" (Romans 8:15)

Sir Archibald the adventurer: "If he would only have admitted that he'd mistaken the means for the end…".

The Grumbling Ghost: "I ought to be alive today and they simply starved me in that dreadful nursing home and no one ever come near me."

The Domineering Spouse: "I'm so miserable. I must have someone to---to do things to."

The Possessive Mother Ghost: "He is mine, do you understand? Mine, mine, mine, forever and ever."

The Lizard-bearing Ghost, Slave to Sin: "It would be better to be dead than to live with this creature."

The Man in a Tragedian Mask: "For a second, he had almost let the chain go, then, as if it were his life-line, he clutched it once more."

What character traits do you display as a heavenly or hellish being?

The Screwtape Letters (1941)

One of the pitfalls of reading *The Screwtape Letters* involves taking C. S. Lewis seriously instead of recognizing his witty irony. The demons attempt to persuade the reader that truth can become false by bending the Word of God, a contemporary issue today for those that twist the gospel and the teachings of Christ for their own satisfaction. Lewis originally called the work, *One Devil to Another*, based upon the dialogue taking place between Wormwood the nephew of Screwtape. The apprenticeship is the art of tempting humans to practice the wrong idea of Christianity. The Letters are a collection of advice on how Wormwood can divert the path of the Christian believer, the "patient," who is experiencing the disasters of World War II. The new Christian spends time with unbelievers as friends, becomes entangled with the love of a Christian girl, and finally is killed when a German bomb explodes. Unlike Augustine, who was tempted by his association with friends before his true Confession to God, the patient here is involved in a spiritual warfare influencing his spiritual life, just as we are also attacked by the principalities of evil in this world. Lewis points out the same obstacles for a genuine faith in Christianity: backsliding in faith, pretending one is a Christian or what we call a "nominal Christian," continually attempting to rededicate your life to Jesus when you never submitted to Him as Lord, believing in love as human rather than divine, and finally dying without an eternal assurance of Christ in one's life.

The demons believe their realism overcomes the false reality of the Enemy, the Creator of reality. The humans' souls become food for the demons, cattle led to the slaughter, but the irony is the limitation of Satan's power compared to God's omnipotence (Job 1:12, Luke 4:6, 2 Thessalonians 2:7-8). Hell, for C. S. Lewis, is a real place, but Lewis never emphasizes the torture there, only the personality traits of selfishness and loneliness removed from God there. Individuals in Hell experience survival of the fittest, with the stronger preying upon the weak. Furthermore, the bureaucratic life is continued in Hell with the authority of a police state. After all, Lewis was influenced by Adolph Hitler's speeches when writing *The Screwtape Letters*. The purpose of writing the letters for Lewis demonstrates the strength of mind one needs for defending the faith of Christianity, not watering down Christianity with social issues and reforms with the latest "fashions." Christianity can become stale, monotonous, and bureaucratic, and we like sheep can all go astray.

CHAPTER 4

Evangelism: The Roots of Witnessing with Mere Christianity

True Truth of the Trinity

Angling toward the Anglican Trinity:

C. S. Lewis' Triune God and his Implications for Evangelical Theology and Science

C. S. Lewis has influenced many Protestant evangelicals with his approach to Christian doctrines, even as an Anglican believer. Peter Williams, warden of Tyndale House Theological Library in London, views evangelical cooperation among conservative, evangelical United Kingdom believers, regardless of denomination. According to Williams, C. S. Lewis' Anglican background "contains many different strands; the affinity between an evangelical Baptist church and an evangelical Anglican church is far bigger than between a liberal Anglican church and an evangelical Anglican one. Often evangelicals of different denominations have good relationships, collaborating with one another."[218] Evangelicals can use C. S. Lewis's insights for furthering the Gospel and for discipleship, growing closer drawn to the conformed

---

[218] Jane Rodgers, "Church Attendance in London Rising, British Theologian Says" (*Southern Baptist Texan*. November 2016), 3.

image of His Son, with the help of the Holy Spirit. From his doctrine and explanation of the Triune Person God, in *Mere Christianity* and in *Christian Reflections*, to his imaginative presentation of the Trinity in his *Chronicles of Narnia* series, Lewis presents a significant statement and illustrations of the Trinity, emphasizing the personal relationship with God, not a mere theological construction, but a complex, difficult image better understood in practice than in systematic theology. Theology for Lewis, in a sense, is "experimental knowledge":

> Christian theology does not believe God to be a person.
> It believes Him to be such that in Him a trinity of
> persons is consistent with a unity of Deity. In that sense
> it believes Him to be something very different from a
> person, just as a cube, in which six squares are consistent
> with unity of the body, is different from a square...
> Our difficulties about the Trinity are of much the same
> kind.[219]

Simple religions are the "made-up" ones, while Christianity is the "myth made real; the heart of Christianity is a myth which is also a fact."[220] As far as the Trinity is concerned, one "does not leave behind the things you find on the simple levels; you combine them in new ways."[221] He demonstrates his concept of the Trinity with several examples, including cubes, the art of praying to and with the Trinity, being pulled across a bridge toward God, friendship, and characterized in his creatures in Narnia: The Emperor of Deep Magic, Aslan the Son, and the Breath of the Holy Spirit. Even if we cannot imagine a three-personal Being, C. S. Lewis declares, "The thing that matters is being actually drawn into that three-personal life, and that may begin any time—tonight, if you

---

[219] C. S. Lewis, "Christianity and Religion," In *Miracles* (New York: Macmillan Publishing Company, Inc., 1960),75.

[220] C. S. Lewis, *Collected Letters,* Volume 1, edited by Walter Hooper (London: Harper Collins, 2000), 976.

[221] C. S. Lewis, "The Three-Personal God," In *Mere Christianity* (New York: Macmillan, 1943), 142.

like."[222] By angling toward the Trinity, Lewis is offering an invitation evangelically to enter into a personal relationship with the Father, Son, and Holy Spirit.

Lewis learned traditional Christian thought from the church, even though he strayed from Christianity into Agnosticism, mystical Theosophy, and even Atheism in periods of his life. In his later return to the myth made real, Lewis returns to the church for his foundations, but not necessarily the Anglican Church. He disagreed with his Inkling challenger, Own Barfield, who believed in a continual evolutionary process of revelation in the web of human souls. For Lewis, the revelation was a special case, already accomplished by Christ, so the revelation was complete, not a natural progression of evolution. Lewis urges membership in the church with an "organized body which shares his own vision of what is meant by revelation."[223] Although creeds like The Apostle's Creed, the Nicene-Constantinopolitan Creed, the Chalcedonian Creed, and the Athanasian Creed can be foundational with biblical tradition and biblical inspiration,[224] Lewis recognized the creeds of the historical church were groundwork for his examination of the theological principles of the Trinity, seeing our historical experience of God as revealed first in the God of the Hebrews (God the Father), then Christ as the Incarnate Lord (Jesus Christ the Son), and ultimately through the Holy Spirit (the Holy Ghost) working within and through the body of the church. C. S. Lewis knew what it was like to be a "reluctant convert,"[225] and understood the difficulties of explaining the Trinity to the common layperson, not with Apologetics and Philosophy, but with simple analogies and illustrations like allegories and metaphors, part of his literary style in

---

[222] C. S. Lewis, "The Three-Personal God," In *Mere Christianity* (New York: Macmillan, 1943, 140.

[223] Owen Barfield, "Lewis and/or Barfield," In C. S. *Lewis and his Circle.* edited by Roger White, Judith Wolfe, and Brendon N. Wolfe (Oxford: Oxford University Press, 2015), 220.

[224] Michael Bird, *What Christians ought to Believe: An Introduction to Christian Doctrine through the Apostle's Creed* (Grand Rapids: Zondervan, 2016), 13.

[225] David C. Downing, *C. S. Lewis's Journey to Faith: The Most Reluctant Convert* (InterVarsity Press, 2002), 164.

his other writings. He was influenced by the allegorical approaches by G.K.K. Chesterton, by George MacDonald, by Owen Barfield, and Dorothy Sayers. Lewis even learned about the Trinity by arguing with the mystical approach to the Trinity by Charles Williams. This Oxford group, the Inklings, was influential in witnessing to Lewis and aiding his reconciliation to Theism on his journey to personal Christian conviction and conversion. Lewis once wrote, "even adult and educated Christians have problems with the correct interpretation of the Trinity,"[226] assuming there was an absolute Trinity to be correctly interpreted.

First, the correct interpretation begins with the correct definition of the Trinity. Lewis defines God as being "three Persons while remaining one being (God), just as a cube is six squares while remaining one cube (solid body)."[227] This paradox creates confusion for the ordinary Christian layperson who might believe in the heresy of Tri-Personalism or what Lewis calls "Tritheism,"[228] leading the Christian to believe theologically in the separation of God as a person. Again, Lewis returns to the example of a cube, in which six squares are consistent with unity of the body but is different from a square. Using Abbott's classic work, *Flatland*, about different dimensions in perception, Lewis uses a literary device and mathematical, logical entity to argue his point:

Flatlanders, attempting to imagine a cube, would either imagine the six squares coinciding, and thus destroy their distinctness, or else imagine them set out side by side, and thus destroy the unity. Our difficulties about the Trinity are of much the same kind.[229]

Lewis admits all the answers cannot be resolved by human logic: "'Logic!' said the professor half to himself. 'Why don't they teach logic at these schools?' Unless any further evidence turns up, we must assume the truth."[230] Thus, God is revealed to us as being *super*-personal, but

---

[226] C. S. Lewis, *Letters to an American Lady*. (Grand Rapids: Eerdmans, April 17, 1953), 14.

[227] C. S. Lewis, *The Three-Person God, Mere Christianity,* 142.

[228] C. S. Lewis, *Letters to an American Lady*, (April 17, 1953), 14.

[229] C. S. Lewis, *The Poison of Subjectivism, Christian Reflections,* 1943, 79-80.

[230] C. S. Lewis, *The Lion, the Witch, and the Wardrobe, Chronicles of Narnia,* 45.

not impersonal; God is three persons instead of *a* person.[231] Lewis also calls the God of the Trinity "a person and more".[232] The Trinity is Omnipresent: "I allow and insist that the Eternal Word, the Second Person of the Trinity, can never be, nor have been, confined to any place at all: it is rather in Him that all places exist."[233] In addition, the third Person, the Holy ghost or the spirit of God is "what grows out of the joint life of the Father and Son as a real Person, with the union between the Father and Son being such a live concrete thing that this union itself is also a person."[234] However, it will take a personal relationship with Christ to convince Lewis ultimately to be drawn to the Trinity, a personal relationship with Platonic friendship first, then love with his wife, Joy Davidman, and then the personal crisis of encountering death of his spouse, until he finds the true truth, "surprised by joy," by "grief observed" in his own life, observing the suffering of Christ on the cross. His own logical Theism, simply by propositional truth, that "I now believe that God exists, and that Jesus Christ is the Son of God," becomes an obstacle for the special revelation directed by the Holy Spirit to draw him near to Christ, reconciling his suffering and the "problem of pain" in his own life. One must surrender himself or herself to the Creator just as "God Himself, as Son, from all eternity renders back to God as Father by filial obedience the being which the Father by paternal love eternally generates in the Son, just as the Holy Ghost proceeds to give back to the Creator in Heaven also"[235] as we imitate this relationship.

Second, the next correct interpretation involves the nature of Love. It is agape love that holds all the loves (*Phileo, Eros, Sorge*) in unity as expressed by Lewis in his work, *The Four Loves*. Screwtape understands this nature of God in the Trinity: "This impossibility, the Enemy (God) calls love, and this can be detected under all He does and even all He is—or claims to be...He claims to be three as well as one, in order that

[231] C. S. Lewis, *Letters*, August 1962.
[232] C. S. Lewis, *God in the Dock*, 185.
[233] C. S. Lewis, *Miracles*, 155.
[234] C. S. Lewis, *Mere Christianity*, 152.
[235] C. S. Lewis, *The Problem of Pain* (New York: MacMillan, 1962), 90.

this nonsense about Love may find a foothold in His own nature."[236] For Lewis, God is Love, a drama, a dance in which we "play out" our love in an active love for God, our fellow human beings, and God's created universe.[237] Dorothy Sayers' theological perspective on the Trinity resonated with Lewis' dramatic, active and dynamic Trinity. She wrote her own dramas and theological essays concerning the Trinity and Love, including The Zeal of Thy House, *The Man who would be King, The Mind of the Maker*. Her idea of the Trinity calls for a Christian love of one's neighbor, but it also calls for a no less truly Christian love of the work; and for a kind of work that will be lovable by the Christian soul."[238] For Sayers, the creative work of the artist is an analogy of a threefold act of creation, including the Creative Idea of the Father, beholding the entire plan of the work; the Creative Energy or Activity, being incarnate in the bonds of matter in the world, or the image of the Word; and the Creative Power, the work of the indwelling Spirit, one exists with the other equally in the work as the Trinity, expressed in her drama, The Zeal of Thy House. Love is present in the author's attitude toward his work as well as in the love of mankind as an expression of the Christian Trinity:

> This is only another way of saying that the work must be measured by the standard of eternity; or that it must be done for God first and foremost; or that the Energy must faithfully manifest forth the Idea; or, theologically, that the Son does the will of the Father.[239]

Dorothy Sayers presented her ideas of the Trinity to the gathering of the Inklings in Oxford in 1941, influencing C. S. Lewis' own work and conception of the Trinity as the embodiment of Christian Love.

---

[236] C. S. Lewis, *Screwtape Letters* (New York: MacMillan, 1961), 81.

[237] C. S. Lewis, *Mere Christianity*, 153.

[238] Dorothy Sayers, *The Mind of the Maker* (San Francisco: Harper and Row, 1979), 217.

[239] Dorothy Sayers, *The Mind of the Maker* (San Francisco: Harper and Row, 1979), 225.

For Lewis, the Love of the Trinity also is a social economy of Divine Order in society, mirroring the relationship between the Father, Son, and Holy Spirit. This analogy "makes possible the reciprocity of love within the Divine Being."[240] Self-surrender is a part of the Trinity; an order mankind was made to imitate. The Son as God is subject to the Father:

> Love is Gift-Love. The Father gives all He is and has to the Son. The Son gives Himself back to the Father Divine and gives Himself to the world and for the world to the Father, and thus gives the world (in Himself) back to the Father too.[241]

The depth of love, Lewis discovers, is in the bond of marriage between husband, wife, and God, a symbol for the reciprocity of the Trinity. Lewis must transform his love for Joy Davidman from a civil duty to a religious obedience, knowing that the unity of the Trinity is experienced in true love, not "being in love" as a feeling:

> It is a deep unity, maintained by the will and deliberately strengthened by habit; reinforced by (in Christian marriages) the grace which both partners ask, and receive, from God. They can have this love for each other even at those moments when they do not like each other; as you love yourself even when you do not like yourself. They can retain this love even when each would easily, if they allowed themselves, be "in love" with someone else. "Being in love" first moved them to promise fidelity: this quieter love enables them to keep the promise. It is on this love that the engine of marriage is run: being in love was the explosion that started it.[242]

This Gift-Love is *Agape* from God, an absolute essence of God.

240 C. S. Lewis, *The Problem* of *Pain*, 29.
241 C.S Lewis, *The Four Loves* (New York: Harcourt Brace, 1960), 11-12.
242 C. S. Lewis, "Christian Marriage," *Mere Christianity,* Book III, 99.

Lewis disagreed with the agnostic approach to love advocated by another Inkling, Charles Williams. Williams insisted upon the paradoxes of love. We have to enter into the worldly experience of love as a sacrament and discover what love is and what it is not. Williams' theory of affirmation and negation treats God the same way: "This also is thou; neither is this thou."[243] For Lewis, the positive affirmation is *Agape* itself which surrounds spiritually all the other loves, including *phileo, Eros, and Sorge* in his explication of *The Four Loves*. This is the Trinity reconciling all the loves into one unity with many functions. God is at home in the "land of the Trinity"[244] as Sovereign of a far greater realm.

The third element of the Trinity, for C. S. Lewis, is the power of prayer. Prayer is the conduit, the communication between the Christian and the Trinity. The Trinity was formulated in the first place by reconciling the love of the Father with the Son and with the Holy Spirit. The relationships occurring in the love of the Trinity are the basis for seeking communication with the creatures God created in his image, *imago dei*. God spoke the Word and it is through the words that humans pray to God, communicating with the Trinity. As Lewis claims, "I cannot help but pray; otherwise, I would stop living."[245] God is personal in the Trinity when believers relate to him through their prayer life. While we are praying to God, the God beside us (Christ) helps us to pray, and God (the Spirit) prompts or encourages us to pray.[246] For Lewis prayer is request that may or may not be granted by the will of God. In his own witty way, Lewis describes prayer: "It is quite useless knocking at the door of heaven for earthly comfort; it's not the sort of comfort they supply there."[247] Lewis rejects Charles Williams' earthly need for prayer to experience the love of the Trinity:

---

[243] Charles Williams, *He came down from Heaven* (London: Faber and Faber, 1950), 25.

[244] C. S. Lewis, *The Four Loves*, 175.

[245] William Nicholson, *Shadowlands* (New York: Penguin Books, 1991), 78.

[246] Perry C. Bramlen, "C. S. Lewis for the Local Church," In *C. S. Lewis Reader's Encyclopedia*. edited by Jeffrey D. Schultz and John G. West (Grand Rapids: Zondervan, 1998), 410.

[247] C. S. Lewis, *Collected Letters* (Volume 2 December 3, 1959), 290.

Since I have begun to pray, I find my extreme view of
personality changing. My own empirical self is becoming
more important, and this is exactly the opposite of self-
love...The efficacy of prayer is, at any rate, no more of
a problem than the efficacy of all human acts. i.e., if
you say, "It is useless to pray because Providence already
knows what is best and will certainly do it," then why is
it not equally useless (and for the same reason) to try to
alter the course of events in any way whatever?[248]

For Lewis, unlike Charles Williams, God is the First Cause: "Our
act, when we pray, must not, any more than all our other acts, be
separated from the continuous act of God Himself, in which alone all
finite causes operate."[249] Thus, discourse between God and man occurs
at particular times for the man, but not for God since God has set the
course of events and the free will of man from the beginning "inherent
in the great single creative act."[250] Lewis suggests our pre-prayer should
be "May it be the real I who speaks. May it be the real Thou that I speak
to."[251] It is in communion with the church that the Trinity appears to
us through prayer in a personal way with the essence of the Trinity, the
"utterly concrete Person":

Prayer is either a sheer illusion or a personal contact
between embryonic, incomplete persons (ourselves)
and the utterly concrete Person. Prayer in the sense of
petition is a small part of it; confession and penitence
are its threshold, adoration its sanctuary, the presence
and vision and enjoyment of God its bread and wine. In

---

[248] C. S. Lewis, *Collected Letters* (Volume 2, February 21, 1932), 149.
[249] C. S. Lewis, "The Efficacy of Prayer," In *The World's Last Night and other Essays*, 1959, 10.
[250] C. S. Lewis, *Letters to Malcolm: Chiefly on Prayer*, 48.
[251] C. S. Lewis, *Letters to Malcolm: Chiefly on Prayer*, 82.

it God shows Himself to us. What He does is learned
from what He is.[252]

C. S. Lewis captures the art of prayer with the Trinity in his poem,
"Prayer" and relates it to the Trinity, the "One forever":

> Master, they say that when I seem to be in speech
> with you,
> Since you make no replies, it's all a dream
> --One talker aping two...
> And thus, you neither need reply
> Nor can; thus, while we seem
> Two talking, thou art One forever, and I
> No dreamer, but thy dream.[253]

Another approach communicating the Trinity concept to his
audiences, especially valuable for evangelism, is the rhetorical technique
Lewis employed: literary figures of speech like allegory, symbol,
metaphor, personification. Although Lewis has been criticized for his
lack of emphasis of the Trinity in his works, such as the *Chronicles of
Narnia* and in his science fiction trilogy, some illustrations can be offered
where the Trinity is symbolically or allegorically utilized in his works,
especially his literary and fantasy works. Several examples of the Trinity
appear in *The Chronicles of Narnia* series:

> In *The Horse and His Boy*, Prince Shasta's question,
> "Who are you?" is presented to the Thing (or person)
> walking beside him. The response includes three ways
> with three different tones of voice implying the power of
> God, the eternal Word (Christ), and the subtle activity
> of the Spirit. Shastra transforms from a fearful Prince

---

[252] C. S. Lewis, "The Efficacy of Prayer," In *The Atlantic Monthly* (Vl. CCIII,
January 1959), 58.
[253] C. S. Lewis, "Prayer," In *Poems,* edited by Walter Hooper (London: Geoffrey
Bles, 1964). 122-3.

to a leader filled with awe, joy, and wonder for the rest of his days.[254]

Lewis said two of the qualities he gave Aslan, the 'strange and solemn perfume' and the 'light', the 'gold' and 'brightness' of Aslan's mane were suggested by passages about the Holy Grail in Malory's *Morte D'Arthur and Tennyson's Idylls of the King.*[255]

In addition, most interpretations of Aslan as "the king of the wood and the son of the great Emperor-beyond-the-Sea"[256] demonstrate the authority of the Father (Emperor). Aslan arrives over the sea just as the Sprit (Trinity) hovered over the water in Genesis 1. The Deeper Magic from Before the Dawn of Time originates with Aslan, "the Son of the One with whom the Deep Magic originated."[257] Just as Jesus is obedient to the Father, Aslan claims to Lucy, "Do you think I wouldn't obey my own rules?" [258] Jesus, the Son of God, came to fulfill his law, not to abolish it.

Another symbol used by Aslan is his breath representing the Holy Spirit: "Aslan incorporates the Second Person of the Trinity by the use of his breath and the sweet fragrance of the person. Jesus breathed on the disciples and said to them, "Receive the Holy Spirit" (John 20:22). Aslan breathes on statues and brings them to a new life symbolic of the power of the resurrection. The Lion confers upon the animals the ability and gift of speech just as the Holy Spirit gave the Apostles utterances (Acts 2:2-4). In *The Magician's Nephew*, Aslan renews and restores all creatures and the creation: "Narnia, Narnia, Narnia, awake. Think. Speak. Be walking trees. Be talking beasts. Be divine waters."[259]

In addition to fantasy writing, C. S. Lewis refers to the Trinity

---

[254] *The C. S. Lewis Reader's Encyclopedia,* edited by Jeffrey Schultz and John G. West (Grand Rapids: Zondervan, 1998), 410.

[255] Walter Hooper, *C. S. Lewis: A Companion and Guide* (San Francisco: Harper, 1996), 441.

[256] C. S. Lewis, *The Lion, Witch, and Wardrobe* (New York: MacMillan, 1950), 8.

[257] C. S. Lewis, *The Lion, Witch, and Wardrobe* (New York: MacMillan, 1950), 13.

[258] C. S. Lewis, *The Voyage of the Dawn Treader* (New York: MacMillan, 1952), 11.

[259] C. S. Lewis, *The Magician's Nephew* (New York: MacMillan, 1954), 9.

indirectly in his science-fiction collection. Walter Hooper defends Lewis' allusions to the Trinity not as a sign of his weakness, but as his ability to use another avenue or "angle" describing the roles and functions of the Trinity. Lewis worried that the Father, Son, and Holy Spirit could not be pictured and was "beyond his capacity, and it would be hard to argue with this except for his dizzyingly successful descriptions of the two planetary archangels, the Oyeresu of Perelandra and Malacandra in *Perelandra*, Chapter 16."[260] The Oyarsa is the "ruling essence"[261] giving shape to the forms of things, an allusion to the Creator Father. The eldila are angelic beings appearing as spiritual beings of light, and Maleldil, The Lord Ruler, just as Jesus the Son is light. Lewis even creates a Bent Oyarsa of Thulcandra for Satan. The three species of rational beings live in unity together ruled by a universal spirit. The Anglican Priest, E.L. Mascall, upheld Lewis' work, "This is an altogether satisfactory story, in which fiction and theology are so skillfully blended that the non-Christian will not realize that he is being instructed until it is too late, discovery the Mystery."[262] The Mystery is the Trinity of Christianity. For Lewis, his response to planetary colonization in *Out of the Silent Planet* was a false hope of improving the human race for the whole universe, a "scientific hope of defeating death is a real rival to Christianity."[263] Lewis main purpose for writing science-fiction was evangelical. He believed "any amount of theology can now be smuggled into people's minds under cover of romance without their knowing it."[264] In his witty manner, Lewis uses science-fiction not to deceive his audience, but to present a realistic warning: "Adults are not deceived by science-fiction; they can be deceived by the stories in the women's magazines."[265] Modern science-fiction was a reversal of good and evil

---

[260] Walter Hooper. *C. S. Lewis: A Complete Guide to his Works* (San Francisco: Harper Collins, 1966), 438.

[261] C. S. Lewis, *Out of the Silent Planet* (New York: Simon and Schuster, 1938), 70.

[262] E.L. Mascall, "The Christian and the Next War," In *Theology* (April 1939), 304.

[263] C. S. Lewis, *Collected Letters* (July 9, 1939), 166.

[264] C. S. Lewis, *Collected Letters* (July 9, 1939), p.167.

[265] C. S. Lewis, *An Experiment in Criticism,* Chapter 7 (Cambridge: Cambridge University Press, 1961), 68.

for Lewis, assuming "moral thought to be a merely subjective thing like one's taste in food, varying from species to species."[266] This poison of relativistic subjectivity detracted from the absolute values of the Trinity.

How then do we extrapolate Lewis' explanations of the Trinity and apply them to evangelism and discipleship? Lewis' ability as a "story-teller" fits well with our postmodern narrative culture today. Since Lewis recognized the limits of our language, we have to approximate the way one grasps the concept of the Trinity. Of course, Lewis acknowledges he does not have the perfect answer to the Trinity explanation, but with the help of the Holy Spirit, we can offer guidelines for understanding the Trinity, while communicating the good news of the gospel. In Chapter Two of *Mere Christianity*, C. S. Lewis discusses this Three-Personal God by illustrating how the Father, the Son, and the Holy Spirit operate in the life of the Christian:

> An ordinary simple Christian kneels down to say his prayers. He is trying to get in touch with God. But if he is a Christian he knows that what is prompting him to pray is also God: god, so to speak, inside of him. But he also knows that all his real knowledge of God comes through Christ, The Man who was God-that Christ is standing beside him, helping him to pray, praying for him...God is the thing to which he is praying-the goal he is trying to reach. God is also the thing inside him which is pushing him on-the motive power. God is also the road or bridge along which he is being pushed to that goal. So that the whole threefold life of the three-personal Being is actually going on in that ordinary little bedroom.[267]

Whether by theology, poetry, essays, science fiction, fantasy, or simple analogy, C. S. Lewis appeals to a wide range of understanding

---

[266] C. S. Lewis, *Christian Reflections* (Grand Rapids: Eerdmans, 1967), 61.
[267] C. S. Lewis, *Mere Christianity,* 143.

from all levels of comprehension. His depth of understanding the elements of the Trinity reveal spiritual insights using various levels of language for different audiences rhetorically. He has given us several angles for approaching the Trinity from his Anglican perspective but reaches beyond limitations in language and doctrines separating our further understanding of the Trinity with his influence on generations of believers as well as his contributions to evangelism and discipleship in the Christian worldview.

The Philosophical Theology of Scientocracy in the Works of C. S. Lewis[x]

The Kingdom is going to arrive: in this world: in this country.
The powers of science are an instrument.
An irresistible instrument.

The quotation above, uttered by a theological clergyman, sounds like a contemporary criticism calling the hyper-idolatry of science a secular religion, or "Scientism," today. However, it was written by C. S. Lewis as science-fiction and fantasy as part of a trilogy in his novel, *That Hideous Strength*[268]. Dystopian, Utopian countries founded upon scientism are familiar to readers in science fiction like George Orwell's *1984*, Aldous Huxley's *Brave New World* as outcomes of social, genetic engineering, but it was Lewis' reading of H.G. Wells' science fiction like *The Time Machine* and *The Mysterious Island of Dr. Moreau* with its genetic engineering aberrations, inspiring his work in science fiction. Ultimately, the scientist wants to play God in the creation of human beings similar to Mary Shelley's *Frankenstein,* searching for immorality not through the blood of Christ, but through the blood of Bram Stoker's *Dracula.* The nineteenth century writers and thinkers, such as Karl Marx, Sigmund Freud, and Friedrich Nietzsche, desired the creation of

---

[268] [x]Acknowledgement: Dr. John G. West, Vice President and C. S. Lewis Fellows Program Director, and the faculty of the Discovery Institute Center for Science and Culture 2016 Summer Seminar, were influential in providing a fellowship grant for studying and researching C. S. Lewis and Science. His collection of essays, *The Magician's Twin: C. S. Lewis on Science, Scientism, and Society* (Discovery Institute, 2012), provides the basis for this study of Lewis' philosophy of science. I thank Dr. Craig Mitchell, professor of Philosophy, Criswell College, for teaching me the philosophy of science, at the Creation Seminar at Southwestern Baptist Theological Seminary (2015), and Dr. Henry Morris III, director of the Creation Research Institute, for his theological teachings of biblical wisdom at First Baptist Church of Dallas. Dr. Jay Richards and Dr. Peter Kreeft also inspired my pursuit of the ethical outcomes of C. S. Lewis' beliefs at the Acton University conference grant and *Ekonomia* fellowship in 2016.
C. S. Lewis, *That Hideous Strength* (New York: Macmillan, 1965), 29.

a new human in a new society, what C. S. Lewis calls "scientocracy." These are the philosophical and anti-theological roots of trans-valuation of values affecting C. S. Lewis in writing several of his works and developing a philosophy of scientocracy, a warning to the twentieth century reader and beyond. He first coins the term *scientocracy*, in a letter to Dan Tucker on December 8, 1959[269], claiming he was not "anti-science," but opposed *scientism*, "the wrong-headed belief that modern science supplies the only reliable method of knowledge about the world, and its corollary that scientists have a right to dictate a society's morality, religious beliefs, and even government policies, merely because of their scientific expertise"[270].

Lewis recognized the limits of science and the need for morality connected with science in a free society. The epistemological claims of science would be served to the society as a political solution to problem-solving, a consequence of the nineteenth century and twentieth century movements of Freudianism, Darwinism, Behaviorism, Pragmatism and Utilitarianism. From Auguste Comte's *Positivism in Science*, to William James *Principle of Psychology*, to Sigmund Freud's *Civilization and its Discontents*, to B.F. Skinner's *Walden II, Beyond Freedom and Dignity*, and ultimately, the evolution of Darwin's reductionistic materialism, Lewis views the progression of progressive science without the limitations of human and theological morality as checks and balances. We the people become the "scientists' puppets."[271]

The Journey to Narnia: The History of the Philosophy of Science

The history of the philosophy of science spans the dialectic tension between Vitalism-Holism versus Mechanism-Materialism. No wonder

---

[269] C. S. Lewis to Dan Tucker, (Dec. 8, 1959), in *The Collected Letters of C. S. Lewis,* edited by Walter Hooper (San Francisco: HarperSanFrancisco, 2007), Vol. III, 1104.

[270] C. S. Lewis, *The Abolition of Man* (New York: Macmillan, 1955), 86.

[271] C. S. Lewis, "Is Progress Possible? Willing Slaves of the Welfare State," In *God in the Dock: Essays on Theology and Ethics,* edited by Walter Hooper (Grand Rapids: Eerdmans), 314.

C. S. Lewis was drawn to this battle, discovering the paradoxes of modern human attempts to discover all the answers to life, to *Zoe*, the biological life-force, opposed to the death of all life, Nature or *Bios/ Thanatopsis*, in the hands of the scientocratic materialists: "*Nature* in the form of air, water, food, etc., is *Bios*. The Spiritual life which is in God from all eternity, and which made the whole natural universe, is *Zoe*."[272] The similarity to Sigmund Freud's drive for *Eros* or the life-wish, versus *thanatopsis* or the death-wish, is remarkable.[273] The biblical theologian could substitute The Holy Spirit for *Zoe* in Lewis' philosophy of science and Screwtape, the Devil, for *Bios-Thanatopsis*, the ruler of death in this materialistic, fallen world. Screwtape teaches us the humans will give in to the attractions of this materialistic world and the knowledge of empiricism, even the new Christian: "So inveterate is their appetite for Heaven that our best method at this stage, of attaching them to Earth is to make them believe that Earth can be turned into Heaven at some future date by what not."[274] The church certainly has been "McFranchised"[275] with worldly marketing and influences with a Marxist economic deterministic emphasis on productivity, statistics, and quantifying the number of converts and baptisms. Where has the glory to God gone? Most of the original founders of science were pursuing categories of knowledge as "devout men of God,"[276] attempting politics, or eugenics, or "science" or psychology or what to glorify God in everything they said and did (*solei Gloria*).

Before the modern advent of "science," no one theory or definition of science existed. The Pre-Socratic Ionian philosophers (Thales, Empedocles, Anaxagoras, Heraclitus, and Empedocles) viewed the

---

[272] C. S. Lewis, *Mere Christianity* (New York: Macmillan, 1943), 140.

[273] Harvey Solganick, *Theories, Translations, Truths: Sigmund Freud's Search for the Psyche Soul,* Unpublished Dissertation (Arlington: The University of Texas at Arlington, 1998).

[274] C. S. Lewis, *The Screwtape Letters* (New York: Macmillan, 1961), 133.

[275] Thomas White and John Mark Yeats, *Franchising McChurch: Feeding Our Obsession with Easy Christianity* (David C. Cook, 2009).

[276] Rodney Stark, *For the Glory of God: How Monotheism led to Reformations, Science Witch-Hunts, and the End of Slavery* (Princeton University Press, 2003), 162.

earthly bodies of earth, air, fire, and water searching for the reductionist, essence of existence. Looking for external causation of cosmology, these philosophers were challenged by Socrates with an inward examination of consciousness. The lines were drawn in the dialectic tension between materialism and idealism. Democritus, Leucippus, and Lucretius attempted to reduce the world to atoms and the void in the Pre-Socratic universe. For them, the most essential element in the nature of reality is substance or matter (materialism) following these assumptions:

> Our sense experience is the source and basis of what we know (empiricism).
>
> Everything can be reduced to atoms and the void (atomism).
>
> Death is the extinction of personality and individuality. (soul sleep)
>
> History has no purpose, only a linear stream of events.[277]

On the other hand, the Greek Idealists and Realists, Plato and Aristotle, pursued Socratic wisdom of the consciousness, the Mind. Plato used mathematics as higher thinking representing the harmony of the Mind, intuiting philosophically higher Forms of Being. Even Aristotle believed in an "unmoved Mover." For Aristotle, science was *Scio*, in Latin, to wonder, to know. However, the pre-modern philosophers of science did not have a dichotomy between faith and reason; their faith in knowing or "science" was not differentiated between philosophy, science and mathematics. Thus, science began in the pre-modern period of the

---

[277] Harvey Solganick, "How your Christian Worldview wins over other Whirled Views:
Naturalism/Materialism" (1 Corinthians 2: 9-14), Bible Study, First Baptist Church of Dallas (Dallas:
January 28, 2015).

Greeks since they had advanced technology such as building technology, astronomy, medicine (brain surgery), mathematics, etc.

This unity of faith and reason strengthened in the medieval period of Scholasticism. Aquinas, Anselm, and Augustine continued the Platonic/ Aristotelean quest of knowledge with biblical wisdom, natural law, and logic.

The modern period of the Enlightenment continued from the so-called "Dark Ages" of the middle ages, since there was no break in the myth of the decline of thinking in the Medieval period, demonstrated by Rodney Stark in *The Glory of God*. However, one demarcation did take place in the history of the philosophy of science. The presuppositions changed:

> The moderns separated faith from reason
> The moderns operated with a hermeneutic of doubt
> Science was seen as superior to faith
> Some thought that science was the only legitimate kind of knowledge
> Some argued that science would replace superstition
> Some argued that science could provide the answers to everything.[278]
> For example, Francis Bacon wrote *The Advancement of Learning*[279].

He argued that scientific knowledge results from continuously experimenting. Observation and experimentation is the key to knowledge of the natural world. The inductive method of empirical probability is exalted above the deductive certainty of the Scholastic Medievalists. The resulting Scientism is the belief that all that can be known, must be known through the scientific process. Even Rene Descartes, an extreme rationalist, turned to empirical investigation of the pineal gland in dissected animals, believing the soul resided there[280]. Anything that cannot be known through the scientific process is nonsense. This scientism is the

---

[278] Craig Mitchell, "The Philosophy of Science," Creation Seminar (Fort Worth: Southwestern Baptist Theological Seminary, 2016).

[279] Francis Bacon, *The Advancement of Learning* (Leopold Library, 2016).

[280] Rene Descartes, *A Discourse of a Method for the Well Guiding of Reason - and the Discovery of Truth in the Sciences* (Hackett Publications, 1999).

main objection to science made by C. S. Lewis. Most who hold this position are not scientists at all. The scientists who hold this position are generally naturalists and reductionist materialists, or what Jay Richards calls "tyrannical materialists," whose small, minute rules gradually soften the will of men with a sincerely exercised tyranny for the sake of victims, are the most oppressive[281]. C. S. Lewis saw this tyranny not only in the wars of the world, but in the political and social application of the scientific-technocratic emphasis of a faith shift to scientism.

The culmination of Scientism occurs in the nineteenth century. The philosophical turn toward consciousness-raising into synthetic knowledge creates a new science approach for higher criticism and rationalism beyond the finite empirical analytical categories of Immanuel Kant[282]. Edmund Husserl searches for a new scientific approach for unbiased human subjectivity with his theory of Phenomenology[283]. Auguste Comte creates a philosophy of society called Positive Science or Positivism[284]. Friedrich Nietzsche thought that there is no objective truth[285]. He also believed that the world picture that physicists construct differs in no essential way from the subjective world picture. Science is just another will to power, a view continued by Mikel Foucault in the post-modern world of the current century[286]. Science cannot get to "the truth" because there is no "truth." Although the logical positivists of the twentieth century advocated a pure objective truth of the scientific methods of investigation: logic, experimentation, language analysis (Wittgenstein),

---

[281] Jay Richards, "Crony Capitalism" (Grand Rapids, MI: Acton University, June 17, 2016).

[282] Immanuel Kant, *Religion on the Grounds of Reason Alone* (Hackett Publishing, 2009).

[283] Edmund Husserl, *Crisis of European Sciences and Transcendental Phenomenology: An Introduction to Phenomenological Philosophy* (Evanston, IL: Northwestern University Press, 1970).

[284] Auguste Comte, *Introduction to Positive Philosophy* (Hackett Publishing, 1988).

[285] Friedrich Nietzsche, *The Gay Science* (*The Joyful Wisdom*) (Vintage Books, 1974).

[286] Mikel Foucault, *Power/Knowledge: Selected Interviews and Other Writings* (Vintage Books, 1980).

and mathematics (Carnap) against the emotivism of humanity (Ayer), by the twenty-first century, science points to no objective truth; instead the Einsteinian and Darwinian theory of relativity and evolution, existential revolt (Sartre, Camus, Kierkegaard), and Heisenberg uncertainty principle lead the new scientism. Post-modernity does not put faith and science in opposition, because it allows for the supernatural, mysticism, in the New Age approach to science and knowledge, the same mysticism C. S. Lewis pursued in Theosophy in his younger years. Thus today, the question philosophically is not between faith and reasoning in science, but realism and anti-realism. Scientific Realists believe that science gets to "the truth," while Scientific Anti-Realists believe that science does not get to "the truth." For example, in the Enlightenment, David Hume was a scientific anti- realist because of his argument against causation: One can know that one thing follows another, but one cannot know that one thing causes another. By the twentieth century, Thomas Kuhn wrote *The Structure of Scientific Revolutions*[287]. He argued that science is really about power. Younger scientists test the existing paradigm with anomalies, while older scientists maintain the status quo and hold on to power. In concluding our observation of the history of scientific philosophy, science does not and cannot provide all of the answers as a scientism. Science is capable of doing many things well, but it cannot test the supernatural. Some things that are viewed as scientific actually are not scientific at all. When science appears to conflict with faith, we should wait until all the test data is in before it should change our beliefs. We should always put faith over "science." We are moving toward too much science, or scientism, radical empiricism and materialism influencing our society, or too little science, toward mysticism, New Age beliefs, and a New Atheism. Both movements were recognized by C. S. Lewis in his works in his returning to a true truth, a true way of knowing, a true "science."

A Philosophy of Science in the Works of C. S. Lewis

---

[287] Thomas Kuhn, *The Structure of Scientific Revolutions* (Chicago: University of Chicago Press, 2012).

Throughout the works of C. S. Lewis, the philosophical inquiry into the nature of "science" interests the author in the advent of the scientific age of the twentieth century. Scientific discovery and wonder are pursued in poetry, essays, theology, apologetic argumentation, as well as in fantasy and science-fiction. Although Lewis did not compose a systematic philosophy of science, the reader can extrapolate some philosophical intuitions in the traditional philosophy of science areas: Metaphysics, or cosmology and ontology; Epistemology, or the scientific methodologies (empiricism, deductive and inductive logic, etc.); Ethics, or the axiological application of a philosophy of science into the value systems; Social and Political Philosophy, or application into the politics and social engineering of science. Each of these categories will be examined according to the primary works of C. S. Lewis for support.

I. Metaphysics

A. Ontology: anti-materialism reduction

C. S. Lewis insists on escaping scientific "dogma" of a physical limited creation of the universe and the existence of matter in the world. He would even agree today with quantum mechanics and the search for an infinite answer with intelligent design implicit in the matter of the universe. In "Dogma and the Universe" (1943), he admits the logical world of causation:

> If anything emerges clearly from modern physics, it is that nature is not everlasting. The universe had a beginning and will have an end. But the great materialistic systems of the past all believed in the eternity, and thence in the self-existence of matter.[288]

However, we must be on guard against physical reductionism since "we all have Naturalism in our bones and even conversion does not at

---

[288] C. S. Lewis, "Dogma and the Universe," In *God in the Dock* (1943) (Grand Rapids: Eerdmans, 1970), 39.

once work the infection out of our system. Its assumptions rush back upon the mind the moment vigilance is relaxed."[289] Lewis will return to the scientific metaphor of "infection" again in *Mere Christianity*, calling Christianity the good infection or contagious Christianity.

B. Cosmology: existence and the infinite universe

C. S. Lewis looked beyond materialistic reductionism in his cosmology. He believed in a real universe created by the Creator; however, the universe went beyond the matter so cherished by evolutionists. In fact, if the universe is turned over to the dominion of man without God's will, mankind will ultimately destroy the universe. In *God in the Dock* (1946), the choice is between the animal world and the spiritual world, racing with the will of God:

> The Christian and the Materialist hold different beliefs about the universe. They can't both be right. The one who is wrong will act in a way which simply doesn't fit the real universe. Consequently, with the best will in the world, he will be helping his fellow creatures to their destruction.[290]

If we worship Nature like a God or as Everything, Lewis asks about our picture or worldview of reality: "How could you ever have thought that this was the ultimate reality? If we are immortal, and if she is doomed (as the scientists tell us) to run out and die, we shall miss this half-shy and half-flamboyant creature, this ogress, this incorrigible fairy, this dumb witch."[291] However, theologians tell us she will be redeemed like ourselves, unlike the naturalists who believe Nature is all that exists as an accident, and will be extinct, with all life banished without possibility of return.[292]

---

[289] C. S. Lewis, *Miracles*, Chapter 17, (1947) (New York: Macmillan, 1978), 164.
[290] C. S. Lewis, "Man or Rabbit?" In *God in the Dock* (1946) (Grand Rapids: Eerdmans, 1970), 110.
[291] C. S. Lewis, *Miracles,* Chapter 9, (1947) (New York: Macmillan, 1978), 66.
[292] C. S. Lewis, "On Living in an Atomic Age" In *Present Concerns: Essays by C. S. Lewis,*1948,74.

Lewis views not "Mother Nature," to be worshipped, but a "Sister" to us to be redeemed.

II. Epistemology

A. Assumptions and Presuppositions

Naturalism is an innate tendency in humans like an original genetic sin of Adam: "We all have Naturalism in our bones and even conversion does not at once work the infection out of our system. Its assumptions rush back upon the mind the moment vigilance is relaxed."[293]

The Laws of Nature do not cause anything to happen; they are a pattern to which every event must conform, induced to happen by the Creator:

> The laws of physics, I understand, decree that when one billiards ball (A) sets another billiard ball (B) in motion, the momentum lost by A exactly equals the momentum gained by B. This is a *Law*. That is, this is the pattern to which the movement of the two billiards balls must conform. Provided, of course that something sets ball A in motion. The *law* won't set it in motion.[294]

B. Principles of Verification

But Nature is not our teacher; it points toward the glory of God in natural revelation:

> "A true philosophy may sometimes validate an experience of nature; an experience of nature cannot validate a philosophy. Nature will not verify any theological or metaphysical proposition; she will help to show what it means."[295]

---

[293] C. S. Lewis, *Miracles,* Chapter 17, (1947) (New York: Macmillan, 1978), 164.
[294] C. S. Lewis, "The Laws of Nature," In *God in the Dock* (1945) (Grand Rapids: Eerdmans, 1970), 77.
[295] C. S. Lewis, *The Four Loves* (1960), Chapter 2 (New York: Harcourt Harvest, 1971), 35-7.

III. Applied Ethics

If Naturalism and Materialism are the only values that exist as a meaningless play of atoms in space and time, producing accidently things like ourselves, Lewis suggest three choices for us:
1. You might commit suicide.
2. You might decide simply to have as good a time as possible—grab the coarsest sensual pleasures.
3. You may defy the universe and go down fighting living according to human values.

But Lewis proposes a spiritual world,

> Suppose we really are spirits and not the offspring of Nature, then we do not have to believe our own minds are chance arrangements of atoms, and then the sciences themselves would be chance arrangements of atoms and we should have no reason for believing them. Instead, we must simply believe we are spirits, free and rational beings, at present inhabiting an irrational universe and must draw the conclusion we are not derived from it. We are strangers here. Nature is not the only thing that exists. We come from another world.[296]

This spiritual world becomes Christianity for Lewis, first as Theism, then as the true truth, Christianity. Natural revelation leads Lewis to a special revelation

A. Axiology: moral rules for living the good life
Classical ethics distinguishes between deontological ethics and teleological ethics. Most scientific systems of ethics rely upon teleological means to an end morality. That is, the pragmatic, utilitarian, and relativistic end justifies the means rather than a duty to the ethical rule

---

[296] C. S. Lewis, "On Living in an Atomic Age," In *Present Concerns: Essays by C. S. Lewis* (1948) (New York: Harcourt Brace, 1987), 75-9.

itself as an absolute moral categorical imperative or deontology. Ethics is a matter of what we "ought to do," or normative, rather than what "is" in a highly objective "scientific" prescriptive rule. In scientific Naturalism, there is no differentiation in ethics concerning ought from is:

> When men say "I ought" they certainly think they are saying something, and something true, about the nature of the proposed action, and not merely about their own feelings. But if Naturalism is true, "I ought" is the same sort of statement as "I itch" or "I'm going to be sick."[297]

Thus, the Naturalist can say "all ideas of good and evil are hallucinations—shadows cast on the outer world by the impulses which we have been conditioned to feel."[298] Lewis emphasizes the epistemic behavioral conditioning of scientists as a warning of "scientocracy" and social engineering in The *Abolition of Man* as well as in his science-fiction trilogy.

B. Social and Political Philosophy

For Lewis, the "Abolition of Man" occurs when the scientists and politicians forget they are human beings affecting other human beings or "men without chests." They hold a philosophy which excludes humanity, yet they remain human. Even at the sight of injustice they throw all their Naturalism to the winds and actually speak like men, unless they forget their humanity. According to Lewis, we continue to make moral judgments believing that the conscience of men is not a product of Nature alone, but is a moral wisdom on its own absolutely, not a product of non-moral, non-rational Nature. The consequences of scientific naturalism, technology, are not the great Teacher; however, Christianity "does not replace technology; when it tells you to feed the hungry, it doesn't give you lessons in cookery."[299] Instead, there is a law of nature based on

---

[297] C. S. Lewis, *Miracles,* Chapter 5, (1947) (New York: Macmillan, 1978), 36.

[298] C. S. Lewis, *Miracles*. Chapter 5, (1947) (New York: Macmillan, 1978), 36-37.

[299] C. S. Lewis, "Answers to Questions on Christianity," In *God in the Dock* (Grand Rapids: Eerdmans, 1970), 48.

objective morality according to Lewis. Scientists must get in touch with their laws written on the heart, not merely following their cultural and political edicts and material grants. They must not become "men without chests," denying objective morals and virtues, and must link their heads with their hearts with true education of confluent emotions and intellect: "They will learn in their education that all emotions aroused by local associations are in themselves contrary to reason and contemptible."[300] These scientists have become conditioned by the Conditioners of society and programmed for the sake of progress alone which ironically will abolish mankind. Lewis warns us: "The heart never takes the place of the head, but can, and should, obey it."[301] The fundamental question in society becomes not which policy is more just, but which group has the most power to impose its will on society or tyranny. Lewis is predating Mikel Foucault's power of the postmodern culture and the Marxist idea of Jurgen Habermas' "special group-consensus power." In the *Abolition of Man*, Lewis emphasizes the "Poison of Subjectivity" and the extreme "Ethical Relativism" dominating the contemporary world: "They may be intending to make a clean sweep of traditional values and start with a new set."[302] The ultimate dystopian society is portrayed in *That Hideous Strength* where science becomes an ally with the tools of government bureaucrats. Instead of Nietzsche's will to power and the *Ubermensch* Superman evolving, the will of the Conditioners will exert their free will over the whole social and political realm with a tyranny of bureaucracy, based upon not true scientific inquiry and discovery, but "scientocracy." Darwinian evolution wins since "there is no ground for placing the preservation of the species above self-preservation or sexual appetite."[303]

Conclusion

---

[300] C. S. Lewis, "Men without Chests," In *The Abolition of Man* (New York: Harper One, 1944), 19.

[301] C. S. Lewis, "Men without Chests," In *The Abolition of Man* (New York: Harper One, 1944), 19.

[302] C. S. Lewis, "Men without Chests," In *The Abolition of Man* (New York: Harper One, 1944), 12.

[303] C. S. Lewis, *The Abolition of Man* (New York: Harper One, 1944), 36.

In his reaction to Physicalism, scientific materialism, naturalism as a cosmology of "scientism" and its application to "scientocracy" in Ethics, Lewis rejects these presuppositions of a philosophy of science and develops a philosophy of science based upon his Christianity:

> When I accept Theology, I may find difficulties in harmonizing it with some particular truths which are imbedded in the mythical cosmology derived from science. But I can get in, or allow for, science as a whole...Reason illuminates finite minds. If, on the other hand, I swallow the scientific cosmology as a whole, then not only can I not fit in Christianity, but I cannot even fit in science... Christian theology can fit in science, art, morality, and the sub-Christian religious. The scientific point of view cannot fit in any of these things, not even science itself.[304]

Theology then is the queen of the sciences.
Biblical Implications of Scientism and Materialistic Naturalism
Natural Man, Spiritual Man, or Carnal Man?

How do we then respond to C. S. Lewis's criticism of scientism, naturalism, materialism or "scientocracy" as evangelical disciples? In Paul's first letter to the Corinthians, he refers to three types of people: The Natural Man, the Spiritual Man, and the Carnal Man. What are these three types of men, and which are you?

First of all, what is the Natural Man? "But the natural man does not receive the things of the Spirit of God, for they are foolishness to him; nor can he know them, because they are spiritually discerned" (1 Cor. 2:14 NKJV). The natural man is the person who does not know Christ. He or she has never been born-again by the Holy Spirit, and therefore the Spirit does not live within. Because the Spirit does not live within, they neither desire spiritual things, nor can they understand them. Paul says

---

[304] C. S. Lewis, "Is Theology Poetry?" In *The Weight of Glory* (1944) (New York: Macmillan, 1980), 91-2.

that the things of God are foolishness to such men. To them, salvation and surrender to Christ are a waste of time. Rather than living for God, they would rather live for self. Ultimately such men will stand before God and be judged for their sin (Rev. 20:11-15 NKJV).

The second type of man Paul refers to is the "Spiritual Man." "But he who is spiritual judges all things, yet he himself is rightly judged by no one. For who has known the mind of the LORD that he may instruct Him? But we have the mind of Christ" (1 Cor 2:15-16 NKJV). Perhaps the most important part of Paul's description of the spiritual man is that he or she "has the mind of Christ." To have the mind of Christ does not mean that we reach a level of perfection or infallibility equal to Jesus. Rather it means that Christ shares with us His spiritual wisdom that enables us to see life from a heavenly perspective and therefore make decisions that are wise for both now and eternity.

How does someone become a spiritual man? First of all, to become a spiritual man, someone must be born-again by the Holy Spirit (John Chapter 3). But that is not all. The spiritual man is also someone whose life is under the control of God's Spirit. Notice what Paul writes -

> But as it is written: "Eye has not seen, nor ear heard, nor have entered into the heart of man the things which God has prepared for those who love Him." But God has revealed them to us through His Spirit. For the Spirit searches all things, yes, the deep things of God. For what man knows the things of a man except the spirit of the man which is in him? Even so no one knows the things of God except the Spirit of God. Now we have received, not the spirit of the world, but the Spirit who is from God, that we might know the things that have been freely given to us by God. (1 Cor. 2:9-12 NKJV)

Through the indwelling presence of the Holy Spirit, God reveals to us His deep spiritual truths. Such truths include God's plan of salvation as well as how to live the Christian life. The spiritual man is someone who is a Spirit-led man.

But there is a third type of man Paul describes, and he is the "Carnal Man." Warren Wiersbe in his *New Testament Commentary* describes the carnal man as – "the immature Christian, the one who lives on a childhood level because he will not feed on the Word and grow." Paul said this of the carnal man –

> And I, brethren, could not speak to you as to spiritual people but as to carnal, as to babes in Christ. I fed you with milk and not with solid food; for until now you were not able to receive it, and even now you are still not able; for you are still carnal. For where there are envy, strife, and divisions among you, are you not carnal and behaving like mere men? (1 Cor. 3:1-3 NKJV)

The word "carnal" means – "fleshly." When applied to a Christian, it means someone, who although they are born-again, they are still allowing their flesh to control much of the way they live and think. Paul called the believers at Corinth "carnal" because they were still acting spiritually immature. Rather than bearing the Spirit's fruit of love, joy and peace, these believers were yielding to old fleshly emotions, such as envy, strife, and division. Notice also that Paul says – "Are you not carnal and behaving like mere men?" or, in other words – "are you not living like men who do not even know the Lord?"

Only God knows for sure whether a carnal man is born-again or not. Rather than judging other men, you and I should be judging ourselves. Though we may not be doing some of the things others might do, are there things in our lives that are displeasing to the Lord? Is there carnality to our Christianity that needs correcting? It is God's will that every believer lives not as the "carnal man," but rather as the "spiritual man."

Implications for Evangelism and Discipleship

What lessons can we learn about the future of our materialistic, scientific, and technocratic world rejecting the Trinity from C. S. Lewis? How can we apply his life discoveries to a model for evangelism and discipleship?

1. Avoid the stumbling blocks of the materialistic world: "Woe to the world because of its stumbling blocks! For it is inevitable that stumbling blocks come; but woe to that man through whom the stumbling block comes! If your hand or your foot causes you to stumble, cut it off and throw it from you; it is better for you to enter life crippled or lame, than to have two hands or two feet and be cast into the eternal fire. If your eye causes you to stumble, pluck it out and throw it from you. It is better for you to enter life with one eye, than to have two eyes and be cast into the fiery hell" (Matthew 18:7-9 NASB).

2. Avoid the confusion of the material brain with the ideas of the mind. The mind gives order (logos) to our thoughts and values to our life, not just synapses in the brain cluster: "Thanks be to God through Jesus Christ our Lord! So then, on the one hand I myself with my mind am serving the law of God, but on the other, with my flesh the law of sin" (Romans 7:25 NASB).

Discovering the Science-Fiction Works by C. S. Lewis

The Science Fiction Trilogy-That Hideous Strength, Out of the Silent Planet, Perelandra

Pilgrim's Regress (1930-1940)

Another indirect approach to evangelical discipleship for Lewis employs science-fiction as a genre for readers. One step away from fantasy is the realm of science fiction. C. S. Lewis loved approaching Christianity through science fiction since it is out of this world in its explorations of other planets and kingdoms and brings the imagination into a search for other worlds. He admits he is unconsciously bringing the reader into an engagement with evangelism even though the reader reads for sheer enjoyment and fantasy. Lewis was influenced by reading David Lindsey's Arcturus, a science-fiction adventure with a spiritual theme. J.B.S. Haldane's *Possible Worlds* also led Lewis to explore how science-fiction could be used as a counter-position defending Christianity, an apologetic ploy by Lewis. Another prevalent theme in his science fiction responds to the scientism developed during the War with its experimentation. Weston becomes a physicist but also a vivisector of animals and eugenics, experimenting on breeding humans through genetic engineering. One only need think of Hitler's experiments during the War. In addition, Weston does not need the classics and history anymore, calling them "trash history." N.I.C.E. in That Hideous Strength becomes the National Institute for Coordinated Experiments. Lewis also includes fantastic beings like Hrossa, Scorns, Pfifltriggi, three intelligent species of Malacandra. He then infuses a pagan god, a Christian reincarnation of a pagan god named Eldil, who represents union in marriage from Venus as well as a war god, Mars, for the guardian of peace. The Christian values of love and peace underlie the message of his science fiction trilogy. Ransom, the hero, becomes a ransom for the many willing to give up his life just as Christ does.

CHAPTER 5

Discipleship and Evangelism: The Roots of Becoming a Mature Christian

We have seen on this journey from the childhood of C. S. Lewis to his death, the reluctant convert met several obstacles for becoming a mature Christian, just as we encounter trials and tribulations in our own journey, as foreigners in a strange land, as aliens searching for truth in a limited kingdom, a science-fiction adventure through *Perelandra*, or a fantasy trip through Narnia. Lewis's beautiful, romantic notion of childhood with two parents and a beautiful garden environment was juxtaposed with the loss of his parents, a war-torn world and the loss of his friend in combat, the alienation of his brother during his education, and the loss of his wife. In all these cases, the great equalizer was the alienation, the deprivation of friendship and relationships, and the abyss of losing one's spirituality and innocence as a child. Lewis attempted to confess his sin by intellectual inquiry, by his questioning atheism, leading to agnosticism and mysticism, and leading him to Theism as an academic understanding of Christianity. Not until he recognizes the cross with a God who suffered pain and sacrificed Himself for others, not himself, does Lewis have a special revelation of Jesus Christ on a personal, relational level. His apologetics allowed Lewis's argument for Jesus as liar, lunatic, or Lord, but his personal journey through the dark night of the soul allowed Lewis to return to his first love as an innocent child and to the doctrines of his creedal beliefs with personal conviction, not just academic comprehension. Thus, Lewis experienced in a special way, the justification of Christ for his salvation on the cross, the sanctification of growing more mature in the image of Christ through his literature and works, but ultimately, the glorification of the expectations, the hope of heaven, not the eternal separation from God in Medieval descriptions of hell, removing the weight of glory in this world as a vapor of reality. Through the evangelical witness of strong friendships, loving relationships, and even enemies of Christianity by arguing the faith with apologetics during his maturation, Lewis establishes a horizontal fellowship with Christ, but it is his special revelation of a vertical relationship with God that opens the entrance of the wardrobe into a revelation of heaven.

Living a Literary Life: The Influence of the Christian Writers— Medievalists and Inklings

The Socratic dialogue of the Inklings in Oxford allows Lewis to explore the world of the imagination, whether it is the influence of Owen Barfield's and Charles Williams' mystical Theosophy, the atheism and agnosticism of social scientism, the language analysis of Dyson, the mythological fantasies of Tolkien, the Orthodoxy of Chesterton, the Medievalist classicists like J.A.W. Bennett, or even the dramatic insights of Dorothy Sayers and Neville Coghill. John Wain, a member of the Inklings, calls the group, " a circle of instigators, almost of incendiaries, meeting to urge one another on in the task of redirecting the whole current of contemporary art and life."[305] Lewis was a Medieval scholar, influenced by Chaucer, Dante, but also dialogued with the Inklings about imaginative literature (fantasy, allegory, mythopoetic tales), Christian philosophy and theology, comparative mythology, Beowulf, Spenser, Milton, courtly love, fairy tale and epic, and language analysis. Their meetings at Magdalen College as well as at the Eagle and Child pub became a model for Socratic inquiry outside the spires of the Oxford classroom. They were creating an evangelic atmosphere for evangelism and discipleship, applying the questioning spirit of the imagination to the world seeking truth. Little did they know the Inklings were recapturing the Medieval Age for a New Age by engaging in apologetics, a defense of the Christian faith, against the contemporary world of mechanism, scientism, materialism, atheism, nihilism, secularism, mysticism, and mankind at war with one another. A hope of returning to Christian virtues could forestall the *Abolition of Man* in the future.

---

[305] Philip Zaleski and Carol Zaleski, *The Fellowship: The Literary Lives of the Inklings: J. R. R. Tolkien, C. S. Lewis, Owen Barfield, Charles Williams* (New York: Farrar, Straus, and Giroux, 2015), 5.

Apologetics: The Roots of Becoming a Logical Christian against New Age Theosophy and Secularism

It is not enough to argue philosophically or intellectually for the sake of argument, but for the sake of a higher foundational principle, *Mere Christianity*. The choices in our contemporary world are threefold: Secularism with its Atheism, Materialism, and high value of Scientism; Mysticism, or New Age spiritualism with its occultism, Orientalism, reincarnation; or Christianity, with its biblical foundations and virtues. Having explored Secularism and New Age mystical beliefs, Christianity has to be the foundational precept for exploring other worldviews (1 Peter 3:16). Without Lewis's absolute knowledge of a reality based on Christianity, we are relativists, situationists, and adrift in a sea of ideas. Apologetics demands a rigorous background in philosophical worldviews and a disciplined study of God's Word in the Bible, reflected in sound doctrines and creeds based upon God's revealed Word. In order for the myth to be made real, language analysis, logic, rationality, and application of knowledge for comprehension, coherence, and consistency must be pursued. However, without the help of the Holy Spirit's guidance, the knowledge of mankind is limited. The same helper helps us in evangelism, discipleship, and becoming more like Christ in our loving approach to encountering those who believe in Secularism or Mysticism. This is our Great Commission (Matthew 28:1). Lewis accomplished an evangelical, apologetic approach to discipleship for us as a model for the Great Commission (Matthew 28:1), spreading the gospel of our Lord, Jesus Christ, through his literary approach, essays, and common-sense practicality.

Implications for Evangelism and Discipleship

What lessons can we learn from the life and works of C. S. Lewis? How can we apply his life discoveries to a model for evangelism and discipleship?

1. *Evangelism is part of your discipleship.* You are fulfilling obedience to Christ evangelizing, as you are becoming conformed to His image by discipleship training. You must be discipled with the disciplined study of God's Word, acquiring the gospel or "good news." C. S. Lewis studied the Bible as well as the doctrines of the church. Our duty is the same duty Christ believed, "The Son of Man has come to seek and to save that which was lost" (Luke 19:10), so we too follow Christ's obedience, "As my Father has sent me, even so send I you." C. S. Lewis established friendships and relationships and extended his love to others, extending the Great Commission, "go and make disciples of all nations" (Matthew 28:19). Most of all the outcome of evangelism and discipleship establishes intimate, transparent relationships built upon Christ's love, a love expressed in the reconciliation of the Trinity.

2. *A philosophical understanding of worldviews, especially a Christian worldview of Mere Christianity, and the ability of defending the gospel and the faith with apologetics are essential for evangelizing and reflecting our growth in discipleship to others.* We can use the literature and life of C. S. Lewis as examples for demonstrating our faith through our own lifestyles, extraordinary actions, testimony, everyday illustrations, quoting Scripture, raising questions, establishing personal relationships. Most of all, we must not neglect the emphasis upon prayer and the reliance we have on the Holy Spirit to guide us in evangelism and discipleship.

3. *We should establish evangelical relationships and discipleship study groups with people from all walks of life, from children, to adolescents, to college age, to singles, to marrieds, to family members, friends, co-workers, couples, neighbors, classmates, and let us not hesitate to engage strangers.* C. S. Lewis experienced all these relationships growing up and even reached out to strangers on his radio broadcasts. The social context of

relationships opens a door for evangelism, but discipleship allows the door to remain open and not shut to new expressions of Christianity for different people's needs and connections. Individual evangelism can lead to community Christianity as well, and vice-versa, since Lewis conversed with the Christians in his micro-community of the Inklings, leading to his step toward his own conversion.

4. *We should never fear nor give up if others are involved in another religion, from another race, class, gender, or sexual orientation.* Christianity is a religion of hope for the lost since Christ wanted all people to come to Him. Usually, people are drawn to Christ (Lewis's *Sehnsucht*) by life situations, no matter how troublesome. We have to remove barriers to plant the mustard seed and allow the Holy Spirit to work on their convictions. Our efforts at evangelism and discipleship will not be sufficient unless they are directed by the Spirit of God who "searches all things, even the deep things of God" (1 Corinthians 2:10). Witnessing to Jewish believers, I had to remove the guilt associated with the holocaust survivor mentality and with losing so many Jewish marriages to Christian marriages. Each circumstance has its own cultural biases and obstacles as challenges.

5. *An understanding of church history, traditions, and doctrinal study will increase our fortitude in presenting the gospel and defending the faith as we grow in discipleship.* C. S. Lewis had a base foundation of the creeds and the traditions of the church before returning to his Christian upbringing from agnosticism, atheism, mysticism, and Theism. The early church fathers and history of the early church establishes a base line for examination to test the spirits. Lewis did not agree with some doctrines like apostolic succession but grappled with the pure doctrines of the church refining his beliefs with questioning and applying rational and experiential wisdom to the precepts of Christianity.

Discovering the Works of Christian Reflection by C. S. Lewis

The Problem of Pain, A Grief Observed, Surprised by Joy

The philosopher, Soren Kierkegaard, centers his whole philosophy upon the art of suffering. Only by suffering, do we experience the emotional depth of the pain Jesus Christ paid on the cross; nothing compares to his sacrificial suffering. Lewis experienced his culmination in suffering the deaths of friends, loved ones, parents, and especially his spouse, whether by war or by cancer. *The Problem of Pain* allows us to work out our suffering moments with what Kierkegaard calls "fear and trembling," allowing our faith to grow exponentially. The combination of his works, *The Problem of Pain, A Grief Observed, and Surprised by Joy*, are, in my opinion, the culmination of Lewis's walk with his faith in Jesus Christ. They are records of his growing pains, counting it all joy in his suffering. This is the cost of discipleship for the Christian, and I hope you have studied the works and life of C. S. Lewis as a model for evangelical discipleship and apologetics of the Christian faith. Lewis has indirectly shared his life and faith with his works, but it is up to us to carry on his work as evangelical, apologetic disciples for the glory of our Lord, Jesus Christ. It is our great commission, our great hope, and our boundless joy as we travel on this journey together from the gardens of *Boxen* to the promised land of *Narnia*.

BIBLIOGRAPHY

Armani, Nicholi. *The Question of God: C. S. Lewis and Sigmund Freud Debate God, Love, Sex, and the Meaning of Life.* New York: Free Press, 2002.

Armani, Nicholi. *The Question of God: School Days. PBS documentary.* 2005. (Accessed 4 November 2005). http://www.pbs.org/wgbh/questionofgod/transcript/school.html .

Atkinson, R.J.C. *The Prehistoric Temples of Stonehenge and Avebury.* London: Pitkin Pictorials, Inc., 1980.

Bacon, Francis. *The Advancement of Learning.* Leopold Library, 2016.

Baier, Kurt. *Problems of Life and Death: A Humanist Perspective.* Prometheus Books, 1997.

Barfield, Owen. "Lewis and/or Barfield." In C. S. *Lewis and his Circle.* eds. Roger White, Judith Wolfe, and Brendon N. Wolfe. Oxford University Press, 2015.

Barfield, Owen. The Case for Anthroposophy. In *The Barfield Reader.* ed. by G.B. Tennyson, 151-52. Wesleyan University Press, 1999.

Barratt, David. *Narnia: C. S. Lewis and His World.* Kregel, 2005.

Bastien, Joseph W. *Mountain of the Condor: Metaphor and Ritual in Andean Aliyu.* St. Paul: West, 1978.

Bird, Michael. *What Christians ought to Believe: An Introduction to Christian Doctrine through the Apostle's Creed.* Grand Rapids: Zondervan, 2016.

Bradley, Marion. *The Mists of Avalon.* London: Sphere Books, Ltd.,1982.

Bramlen, Perry C. C. S. Lewis for the Local Church. In *C. S. Lewis Reader's Encyclopedia*. eds. Jeffrey D. Schultz and John G. West. 410. Grand Rapids: Zondervan, 1998.

Buber, Martin. *I and Thou*. New York: Scribner's Press, 1970.

Caine, Mary. *The Glastonbury Zodiac: Key to the Mysteries of Britain*. Ashford, England: Flexishape Books, 1978.

Castaneda, Carlos. *The Fire Within*. New York: Simon and Schuster, 1984.

Castaneda, Carlos. *The Teachings of Don Juan*. New York: Simon and Schuster, 1984.

Chase, Mary. *Harvey*. Snowball Publishing Company, www.snowballpublishing.com (August 20, 2014), 1944.

Chesterton, G. K. *The Everlasting Man*. Ignatius, 2000.

Christenson, Michael J. *C. S. Lewis on Scripture: His Thoughts on the Nature of Biblical Inspiration, The Role of Revelation, and the Question of Inerrancy*. Word Publishers, 1979.

Clifford, Marcus and J., eds. *Writing Culture*. Berkeley: University of California Press, 2012.

Cofffman, Elesha. "Profiles in Faith: G.K. Chesterton." *Knowing and Doing*. 3. Redlands, California: C. S. Lewis Institute, 2005.

Coleman, Loren. *Curious Encounters: Phantom trains, Spooky spots, and other Mysterious Wonders*. Winchester, MA: Faber and Faber, Inc., 1985.

Comte, Auguste. *Introduction to Positive Philosophy*. Indianapolis, IN: Hackett Publishing, 1988.

Coren, Michael. *The Man who created Narnia: The Story of C. S. Lewis*. Grand Rapids: Eerdmans, 1996.

Cowan, Steven B., ed. *Five Views on Apologetics*. Grand Rapids: Zondervan, 2000.

Craig, William Lane and Walter Sinnott-Armstrong. *God: A Debate between a Christian and an Atheist*. Oxford: Oxford UP, 2004.

Descartes, Rene. *A Discourse of a Method for the Well Guiding of Reason - and the Discovery of Truth in the Sciences.* Indianapolis, IN: Hackett Publications, 1999.

Dominquez, Virginia. *People as Subject; People as Object*. Madison: University of Wisconsin Press, 1989.

Dorsette, Lyle and Marjorie Lamp Mead, eds. *C.S. Lewis: Letters to Children*. Macmillan Publishing Company, 1985.

Downing, David C. *C. S. Lewis's Journey to Faith: The Most Reluctant Convert*. InterVarsity Press, 2002.

Downing, David C. *Mysticism in C. S. Lewis: Into the Region of Awe*. Downers Grove, IL: InterVarsity Press, 2005.

Downing, David C. *Into the Region of Awe: Mysticism in C.S. Lewis*. Grand Rapids: IVP. 2005.

Dufrenne, Mikel. *The Notion of the A Priori*. Evanston: University of Northwestern Press, 1966.

Dufrenne, Mikel. *The Phenomenology of Aesthetic Experience*. Evanston: Northwestern Press, 1966.

Dunbar, John G. and Jan Fisher. *Iona*. Edinburgh: Royal Commission on the Ancient and Historical Monuments of Scotland,1983.

Edersheim, Alfred. *The Life and Times of Jesus the Messiah*. Henrickson Publishers, 1993.

Edwards, Bruce. *Into the Wardrobe: C. S. Lewis Website*. http://cslewis. drzeus.net.

Evans, C. Stephan. *Pocket Dictionary of Apologetics and Philosophy of Religion*. Intervarsity Press, 2002.

Foucault, Mikel. *Power/Knowledge: Selected Interviews and Other Writings*. Vintage Books, 1980.

Freud, Sigmund. *The Future of an Illusion*. New York: W.W. Norton, 1989.

Gamwell, Lynn and Richard Wells. *Sigmund Freud and Art: His Personal Collection of Antiquities, Freud Museum, London*. Introduced by Peter Gay. New York: State University of New York, 1989.

Geisler, Norman L. and Frank Turek. *I don't have enough Faith to be an Atheist*. Wheaton, IL: Crossway, 2004.

Gliyer, Diana Pavlac. "Anglicanism." In *C. S. Lewis Reader's Encyclopedia*. 80-81. Grand Rapids: Zondervan, 1998.

Harcourt Christian Standard Bible. Nashville: Holman Bible Publishers, 2004.

Heidegger, Martin. *Language, Truth, and Meaning.* Bloomington, IA: University of Indiana Press, 2016.

Heidegger, Martin. *The Way Back to Metaphysics.* In *Basic Writings.* New York: Harper Perennial Classics, 2008.

Hinton, Marvin D. and Bruce L. Edwards. "William T. Kirkpatrick." In *The C. S. Lewis Reader's Encyclopedia.* 229. Grand Rapids: Zondervan, 1998.

Hippocrates, George Apostle and Lloyd P. Gerson, eds. *Aristotle-Selected Works.* Grinnell: Peripatetic Press, 1991.

Hooper, Walter, ed. *All my Road before Me: The Diary of C. S. Lewis 1922-1927.* Foreword by Owen Barfield. San Diego: Harcourt Brace, 1991.

Hooper, Walter. *C. S. Lewis: A Companion and Guide.* San Francisco: Harper, 1996.

Hooper, Walter. *C. S. Lewis: A Complete Guide to his Works.* San Francisco: Harper Collins, 1966.

Howard-Gordon, Frances. *Glastonbury: Maker of Myths.* Glastonbury: Gothic Image Books, 1982.

Husserl, Edmund. *Crisis of European Sciences and Transcendental Phenomenology: An Introduction to Phenomenological Philosophy.* Evanston, IL: Northwestern University Press, 1970.

Husserl, Edmund. *Ideas (Ideen): General Introduction to Pure Phenomenology.* New Jersey: Routledge Classics, 2012.

Jeffress, Robert. *How can I know? Answers to Life's 7 most important Questions.* Nashville, TN: Worthy Books, 2013.

Jenkins, Palden. *Planetary Paths: Energy Centres, ancient remains, leylines, coast and islands.* Santa Barbara, CA: ABC-CLIO Publishers, 2005.

Kant, Immanuel. *Religion on the Grounds of Reason Alone.* Indianapolis, IN: Hackett Publishing, 2009.

Kort, Wesley. *Reading C. S. Lewis: A Commentary.* Oxford: Oxford University Press, 2015.

Kuhn, Thomas. *The Structure of Scientific Revolutions*. Chicago, IL: University of Chicago Press, 2012.

Kurtz, Paul. *A Humanist Manifesto One and Two*. Amherst, NY: Prometheus, 1973.

Lee, R.G. "The Face of Jesus Christ." In *Payday Someday and other Sermons*. eds. Timothy and Denise George. 68-87. Nashville, TN: Broadman and Holman Publishers, 1995.

Lemmel, Helen H. "Turn Your Eyes Upon Jesus." (1922). http://my.homewithgod.com/heavenlymidis/songboook/turneyes.html

Levi-Strauss, Claude. *Tristes Tropiques: Sad Tropics*. New York: Antheum, 1974.

Lewis, C. S. *The Collected Letters of C. S. Lewis, Vol.1: Family Letters, 1905-1931*. San Francisco: Harper Collins, 2004.

Lewis, C. S. *A Grief Observed*. New York: HarperSanFrancisco, 1989.

Lewis, C. S. *An Experiment in Criticism*. Cambridge: Cambridge University Press, 1961.

Lewis, C. S. *Boxen*. ed. by Walter Hooper. San Diego: Harcourt Brace, 1985.

Lewis, C. S. "Bulverism or the Foundation of 20th Century Thought." *God in the Dock*. ed. by Walter Hooper. 299-304. Grand Rapids: Eerdmans, 1972.

Lewis, C. S. *Christian Reflections*. Grand Rapids: Eerdmans Publishing Company, 1967.

Lewis, C. S. *Dymer*. Canto 15;17. London: J.M. Dent Publications. Distributed by Macmillan, 1926.

Lewis, C. S. *English Literature in the Seventeenth Century excluding Drama*. Vol.4. Cambridge: Oxford Clarendon Press, 1944.

Lewis, C. S. *God in the Dock*. Grand Rapids: Eerdmans Publishing Company, 1970.

Lewis, C. S. "Is Progress Possible? Willing Slaves of the Welfare State." *God in the Dock: Essays on Theology and Ethics*. 314. ed. by Walter Hooper. Grand Rapids: Eerdmans.1970.

Lewis, C. S. "Is Theology Poetry?" *The Weight of Glory*. (1944). 91-92. New York: Macmillan, 1980.

Lewis, C. S. *Letters of Lewis, C. S.* New York: Harcourt Brace Jovanovich, 1966.

Lewis, C. S. *Letters to an American Lady.* Grand Rapids: Eerdmans, 1967.

Lewis, C. S. *Letters to Malcolm: Chiefly on Prayer.* New York: Harcourt, Brace Jovanovich, 1964.

Lewis, C. S. *Mere Christianity.* New York: Macmillan Publishing Company, 1952.

Lewis, C. S. *Miracles: How God intervenes in Nature and Human Affairs.* New York: Macmillan, 1940.

Lewis, C. S. "On Living in an Atomic Age." *Present Concerns: Essays by C. S. Lewis.* 75-79. New York: Harcourt Brace, 1987.

Lewis, C. S. "On Three Ways of Writing for Children." In *On Stories and Other Essays in Literature.* ed. by Walter Hooper. New York: Harcourt Brace, 1982.

Lewis, C. S. *Out of the Silent Planet.* New York: Simon and Schuster, 1938.

Lewis, C. S. "Prayer." *Poems.* ed. by Walter Hooper. 122-123. London: Geoffrey Bles, 1964.

Lewis, C. S. *Reflections on Psalms.* New York: Harcourt, Brace, Jovanovich, 1958.

Lewis, C. S. *Screwtape Letters.* New York: Macmillan Publishing Company, 1959.

Lewis, C. S. *Surprised by Joy.* Fort Washington, PA: Harvest Books, 1966.

Lewis, C. S. *Surprised by Joy.* New York: Macmillan, 1955.

Lewis, C. S. *That Hideous Strength.* New York: Macmillan, 1965.

Lewis, C. S. *The Abolition of Man.* New York: Macmillan, 1955.

Lewis, C. S. "The Efficacy of Prayer." In *The Atlantic Monthly* (Vol. CCIII: 58. January 1959).

Lewis, C. S. *The Four Loves: read by the author.* Word Audio Cassette. Dallas: Word Publishing, 1970.

Lewis, C. S. *The Lion, Witch, and Wardrobe.* New York: MacMillan, 1950.

Lewis, C. S. *The Magician's Nephew.* New York: MacMillan, 1954.

Lewis, C. S. "The Poison of Subjectivism." In *Christian Reflections*. 79-80. Grand Rapids: Eerdmans, 1943.

Lewis, C. S. *The Problem of Pain*. New York: Macmillan Publishing Company, 1978.

Lewis, C. S. *The Screwtape Letters*. New York: Collier Macmillan.1982

Lewis, C. S. *The Voyage of the Dawn Treader*. New York: MacMillan, 1952.

Lewis, C. S. *The World's Last Night and Other Essays*. New York: Harcourt Brace Jovanovich, 1960.

Lewis, C. S. *Till We Have Faces*. New York: Harcourt Brace, 1980.

Lewis, C. S. *Till We Have Faces: A Myth Retold*. Grand Rapids: Eerdmans, 1956.

Lindsley, Art. *Profiles in Faith: J.R.R. Tolkien. Knowing and Doing*. Redlands, CA: C. S. Lewis Institute, 2002.

Lombroso-Ferrero, Gina. *Criminal Man, According to the Classification of Caesare Lombroso*. New York, NY: Patterson Smith, 1972.

Macleod, Fiona. *Iona*. Edenborough: Floris Books, 1982.

Malory, Sir Thomas. *LeMorte d'Arthur: King Arthur and the Legends of the Round Table*. Cambridge: Cambridge UP, 1973.

Manser, M.H. *Dictionary of Bible Themes: The Accessible and Comprehensive Tool for Topical Studies*. London: Martin Manser, 2009.

Marples, Morris. *White Horses and other Hill Figures*. Gloucester: Alan Sutton Publishing, Ltd., 2005.

Marx, Karl. *Das Kapital*. New York, NY: Gateway, 1999.

Mascall, E.L. "The Christian and the Next War," In *Theology*. 304. April 1939.

McDowell, Josh. *More than a Carpenter*. Carol Stream, IL: Tyndale House Publishers, 2009.

Merleau-Ponty, Maurice. *Phenomenology of Perception*. Paris: Gallimard, 1945.

Metaxas, Eric. *C. S. Lewis: Mere Christianity*. video. Zondervan, 2016.

Murray, Peter and Linda, eds. "Christ." In *The Oxford Companion to Christian Art and Architecture: the Key to Western Art's most Potent Symbolism.* 103. Oxford: Oxford University Press, 1996.

Nelson, Kai. *Ethics without God.* Amherst, NY: Prometheus, 1990.

Newman, Barbara. "Charles Williams and the Companions of the Co-inherence". In *Spiritus: A Journal of Christian Spirituality* 9 (1): 1–26. doi:10.1353/scs.0.0043. ISSN 1535-3117. January 1, 2009.

Newman, Randy. *Questioning Evangelism: Engaging People's Hearts the Way Jesus did.* Grand Rapids, MI: Kregel, 2004.

Nicholson, William. *Shadowlands.* film. directed and produced by Richard Attenborough. Paramount Pictures, 1993.

Nicholson, William. *Shadowlands.* New York: Penguin Books, 1991.

Nicholson, William. *Shadowlands.* television film. directed by Norman Stone and produced by David M. Thompson for BBC Wales, 1985.

Nietzsche, Friedrich. *The Gay Science (The Joyful Wisdom).* New York: Vintage Books, 1974.

Nietzsche, Friedrich. *Human, All too Human.* Cambridge: Cambridge UP, 1996.

Nietzsche, Friedrich. *Beyond Good and Evil.* New York: New American Library, 1966.

Orwell, George. *1984.* New York: Signet, 1948.

Ovid. *The Metamorphoses.* transl. Anthony S. Kline. http://ovid.lib.virginia.edu/trans/Ovhome.htm

Piggott, Stuart. *The Druids.* London: Thames and Hudson, 1968.

Pike, Mark A. *Mere Education: C. S. Lewis as Teacher for our Time.* Cambridge: Lutterworth Press, 2013.

Pirsig, Robert. *Zen and the Art of Motorcycle Maintenance.* New York: Bantam Books, 1974.

Platonicus, Lucius Apuleius. (125 A.D.). *Metamorphoses.* Ed. Robert Graves. New York: Penguin, 1950.

Richards, Jay. "Crony Capitalism." Lecture. Acton University. Grand Rapids, MI. June 17, 2016.

Ricoeur, Paul. *Hermeneutics and the Human Sciences: Essays on Language, Action, and Interpretation.* Cambridge: Cambridge UP, 1981

Rodgers, Jane. "Church Attendance in London Rising, British Theologian Says." 3. In *Southern Baptist Texan*. November 2016.

Russell, Bertrand. *A Free Man's Worship*. Ephrata, PA: Mosher, 1927.

Russell, Bertrand. *Why I am not a Christian*. Bloomington, IN: Simon and Schuster Touchstone, 1967.

Sammons, Martha. *Guide through Narnia*. Wheaton, IL: Harold Shaw Publications, 1979.

Saussure, Ferdinand. *Course in General Linguistics*. New York: McGraw-Hill, 1965.

Sayers, Dorothy. *The* Mind of the *Maker*. San Francisco: Harper and Row, 1979.

Scott, Clara H. 1895. "Open my Eyes that I may See." www.tagnet.org/digitalhymnal/en/dh326.html

Sharkey, John. *Celtic Mysteries: The Ancient Religion*. New York: Crossroad Publications, 1981.

Sibley, Brian. *Shadowlands: The True Story of C. S. Lewis and Joy Davidman*. Grand Rapids: Baker Fleming H. Revell, 1985.

Sinnett, A.P. *The Pyramids and Stonehenge*. London: Theosophical Publishing House, 1970.

Skinner, B. F. *Beyond Freedom and Dignity*. Indianapolis, IN: Hackett, 2002.

Smith, Steve. *Dying to Preach: Embracing the Cross in the Pulpit*. Grand Rapids, MI: Kregel, 2009.

Solganick, Harvey. *Theories, Translations, Truths: Freud's Search for the Soul*. Heidelberg: University of Heidelberg International University, unpublished manuscript, 1988.

Solganick, Harvey. "Apologetics Worldviews." *Encyclopedia of Christian Civilization*. Blackwell, 2012.

Solganick, Harvey. "C. S. Lewis: Angling toward the Trinity as an Anglican." Evangelical Theological Society National Conference. San Antonio, Texas. November 2016.

Solganick, Harvey. "Naturalism/Materialism" (1 Corinthians 2: 9-14). Bible Study. First Baptist Church of Dallas. Dallas: January 28, 2015.

Solganick, Harvey. "Phenomenal Power Spots." Presentation in Huma 5303: The New Ethnography. Arlington, TX: University of Texas at Arlington. June 30,1994.

Solganick, Harvey. *C. S. Lewis' Influence on Protestant Evangelism and Discipleship*. Sabbatical Grant at C. S. Lewis Institute, England, July 2017.

Solganick, Harvey. *Creative, Constructive, Critical Thinking for the Christian*. Arlington, TX: London Press, 2013.

Solganick, Harvey. *Disciple6: Christianity*. Online. ed. Richard Ross. Southwestern Baptist Theological Seminary. Fort Worth, TX: Seminary Hill Press. 2016.

Solganick, Harvey. *Freud's Search of the Soul: Theories, Translations, and Truths*. Unpublished dissertation. Arlington, Texas: The University of Texas at Arlington, August 1998.

Stafford, Greg. "The Labyrinth and Tor of Glastonbury." 40-43. *Shaman's Drum*. Glastonbury: Summer Edition, 1987.

Stark, Rodney. *For the Glory of God: How Monotheism led to Reformations, Science Witch- Hunts, and the End of Slavery*. New Jersey: Princeton University Press, 2003.

Starr, Nathan Comfort. *C. S. Lewis's Till We Have Faces: Religious Dimensions in Literature*. New York: Seabury Press, 1968.

Stone, Elaine Murray. *C. S. Lewis: Creator of Narnia*. Mahwah, New Jersey: Paulist Press, 2001.

Thiselton, Anthony C. *A Concise Encyclopedia of the Philosophy of Religion*. Grand Rapids: Baker Academic Books, 2002. 18.

Tozer, A.W. "Following Hard after God." In *Pursuit of God*. Camp Hill, PA: Christian Publications, 1982.

Visser, John. ed. *Into the Wardrobe: A C. S. Lewis Website. 1994.* http://cslewis.drzeus.net/\

Wheeler, Sessions S. *The Desert Lake: The Story of Nevada's Pyramid Lake*. Caldwell, Idaho: University of Idaho Caxton Press, 2001.

White, T.H. *The Book of Merlyn: The Unpublished Conclusion to the Once and Future King*. New York: Ace Publishers, 1987.

White, Thomas and John Mark Yeats. *Franchising McChurch: Feeding Our Obsession with Easy Christianity*. Colorado Springs, CO: David C. Cook, 2009.

Williams, Alexandria. 'I Want to See Jesus In Every Song I Sing Today." http://www.geocities.com/alexandria_williams/ Content/ iwanttoseeJesus.htm .

Williams, Charles and C. S. Lewis. *Arthurian Torso*. 143.

https://laurelandelmo.wordpress.com/2013/09/18/arthurian-torso-b y-charls-williams-and-c-s-lewis/.

Williams, Charles. *Arthurian Torso*. London: Oxford University Press, 1948.

Williams, Charles. *He came down from Heaven*. London: Faber and Faber, 1950.

Wilson, A.N. *C. S. Lewis: A Biography*. New York: W. W. Norton, 2002.

Wilson, Walter L. *A Dictionary of Bible Types*. Peabody, MA: Hendrickson Publishers, 1999. 142.

Wood, Robert C. "Conflict and Convergence on Fundamental Matters in C. S. Lewis and J.R.R. Tolkien." published in *Renascence*. (Accessed 15 October 2005) http://www3.baylor.edu/~Ralph_Wood/lewis/L ewisTolkienTension.pdf

Wright, Gordon. *Jura: A Guide for Walkers*. Jura Isle: Sproat Printers, 1983.

Zaleski, Philip and Carol Zaleski. *The Fellowship: The Literary Lives of the Inklings: J. R. R. Tolkien, C. S. Lewis, Owen Barfield, Charles Williams*. New York: Farrar, Straus, and Giroux, 2015.

ABOUT THE AUTHOR

Harvey Solganick, Ph.D. (The University of Texas at Arlington) is the Senior Professor of Humanities and Philosophy at J.R. Scarborough College of Southwestern Baptist Theological Seminary, Fort Worth, Texas. He also serves as Adjunct Professor at LeTourneau University, Dallas Baptist University, Criswell College, and Richland College, Dallas, Texas. Previously, he was Core Coordinator Director and Professor of English and Philosophy, Missouri Baptist University, St. Louis, and chairman of Communications at Eastfield College, Mesquite, Texas. His numerous presentations and publications include articles on C. S. Lewis, Sigmund Freud, and Apologetic Worldviews, as well as a book in Critical Thinking (London Press). He received grants from the C. S. Lewis Foundation, Oxbridge, and from the Discovery Institute Seattle, as a C. S. Lewis Fellow, researching the background for this study on C. S. Lewis. He resides in Dallas, Texas with his spouse, Elaine, who teaches Sociology at Grantham University. Both attend the First Baptist Church of Dallas, where he teaches the Mission Minded Class and serves as an instructor of C. S. Lewis at Discipleship University.

Printed in the United States
By Bookmasters